I
Love
Me

How To Learn To Love Yourself

Paul Hughes

Table Of Contents

INTRODUCTION

The most amazing, life-altering joy that can be experienced is living in a state of constant self-love. While it may at the outset sound idealistic to think this can be a regular when the Gratitude-Abundance formula is in place, it certainly will be. Once this is solid, self-love will always be a reliable staple despite any circumstances surrounding you.

Imagine being beaten up with days full of the worst possible news. Imagine being caught in a whirlwind of chaotic circumstances. Imagine being in those situations and still have an overriding sense of confidence in yourself, with the automatic reaction of always nourishing yourself with care, which you feel is always well-deserved. Imagine being in such circumstances, and knowing there is no way you cannot be okay, as the universe is rigged in your favor. That sense of wellness and knowing sees you through.

I truly thought with all the knowledge I had on mindfulness and self-love that I had that intact, but my actions did not align with my understanding for quite a long time. Of course, I was going through the motions with some sort of action, but I didn't quite get it, did I? How could I say I truly got it when I was depleting myself so much for the benefit of others while portraying what externally may be seen as an exceptional example of being a mindfulness queen? All the mantras and meditations in the world could not save me until I saved myself with the Gratitude-Abundance formula. Therein lies the magic, wonder, and truth of real love.

It is amazing to see what you think you have when your life is in order, based on general knowledge of what order is in the opinion of the masses. I had what could be seen as perfect order in this view for a very long time. It is interesting to see all the people that are in your life when this perfect order exists. People latched onto me and enjoyed soaking up every moment of what was presented as sunshine. Having a core of what seemed to be life-enhancing and healthy friendships was effortless for me. I could do anything I wanted and have anything I wanted, and their people were, right along with me, riding the wave.

When I hit my rock bottom point, my first thought was that, of course, all of these people that had been there all along would be there for me through that as well. I breathed a sigh and said, "At least I have them." After all, they were friends, some of which I considered to be blood. I'd always known we would be old and grey together. There was no doubt in my mind. Besides friends, there were people that had always displayed warmth towards me, and they showered me with adoration and compliments. The great majority of these people in my life proved to not be real when I fell from grace to a scary, uncertain place in my life where I was suddenly at a different status than I'd ever expected could be possible.

There was initially a feeling of unity with the dramatic uprising of my upheaval, as a physical need was met but frankly, in the grand scheme of things overall, I was abandoned emotionally, mentally, and physically. I was no stranger to abandonment in life, but the key here was these were the people that I carefully selected as my precious circle, knowing they would always be there.

The dispersing of my circle followed the abandonment from the partner I gave my all to that committed eternal love to me, which led to hitting rock bottom in the first place. I was abruptly spiraled out of all that I thought to be true and secure and utterly wiped out. Abandonment due to pleading so much for so long for baseline respect within my house; I will never beg again or allow myself to be a victim to constant invalidation and delusion. The subject matter at hand was the teenager I inherited in the marriage, 18 at the time, who I gave strenuously to, but suffered so much disrespect from that through time that draining situation even took away my will to live. Making matters worse, a cleverly crafted false narrative was disseminated to the outside world, and I felt like it was broadcast like a newspaper headline without regard for the truth of my strenuous commitment and the glaring clarity I provided about what was desired.

The new life that reeked of devastation was laughed at directly in my face, and everything around me I was able to regain was diminished with thoughtless, piercing words. Insensitivities abounded, and no matter what I explained, there was no desire for empathy and understanding even to try to relate in any way. There were many times when it was always thrown in my face what a person had and was doing right after the same person denied me of basic human needs that even a stranger would not deny if they saw someone on the street. Not wanting to get involved was offered as an excuse for denying the most basic level of help and disaster evasion, although there was a constant desire for involvement all those years riding the glorious wave of my life of ease, pleasure, and plenty. The trauma of my experience was constantly brought up, and there were even efforts to dig up information to cause a stir, even after setting strong and clear boundaries over and over again. It was so consistent and repetitive that it was overwhelming, besides being talked over empathically with all the merits of my healing and recovery being put in dispute.

Even the people that were not classified as friends that I described as always being warm with high praise for me profoundly let me down. I was told by one that they didn't care to know whether I lived or died, just as long as I provided them with what they needed, which I could no longer do as I previously had while everyone was riding the wave.

Overall, there were words spoken that shocked me all the time. It was all based on not wanting to relate or deeply understand with compassion. I heard I was all of a sudden stupid after all of the successful decades of my life, all of my degrees, all of my achievements, and all of my outstanding displays in a row. In their view, the devastating loss had to mean I wasn't enough anymore as a result of personal flaws – not smart enough, not shrewd enough, without any common sense, and purposely a fumbling idiot, wide-eyed as a deer in headlights. Meanwhile, I was acting with unconquerable character, integrity, and effort better and stronger than I ever had to in my entire life.

I wanted to pull my hair out in exasperation, thinking about how consistently the first 38 years of my life up to that point, I never wavered in showing I had motivation and competence to manage life. I had 38 years of consistent proof that I was the maestro of all things in the sphere of finances and life management. I managed millions at Fortune 500 corporations and was the highest level financial executive for a non-profit, so managing my own life worked like clockwork. I was a businesswoman, thriving at a point, and proud of my ability to innovate in an emerging space, conquer unimaginable complexities, and demonstrate leadership at its best. I was on auto-pilot with a system in place that seemed impenetrable with no view of my Achilles' heel. All they'd ever seen was my constant social engagement, a pipeline of career and personal life achievements, and displays of ease as I thoroughly enjoyed the pleasures offered by life. I had the rug swept up under me, and I wanted acknowledgment that, of course, I had accountability, but it was a simple matter of fact that bad things happen to good people.

I was not expressing my new vulnerability because I needed to be told how to manage life. I was proficient, and all of that knowledge doesn't disappear in the blink of an eye. Yet, there I was, literally crying overnight on a hardwood floor with no bed and my stomach aching with starvation, hearing I was stupid. When an unexpected natural disaster suddenly occurs as a result of a rumbling of the elements, condemning someone for experiencing this would be absurd. Why, then, are fellow human beings treated this way when the rumbling of events causes disaster?

I am not sweeping aside the fantastic support a few gave me. I deeply appreciate and will always hold this in my heart as a cherished memory. I am expressing the gravity of loss here with the 90% that were not real, so we can get to how I transitioned from this state to my self-love 'A' game. What remained in the few was so precious and instrumental to my growth that it is forever an integral part of my very being.

My parents picked me up when I was far down at the bottom without the mocking, disregard for my life, and chastising that I'd experienced. It was a welcome embrace. The depths of love and compassion were at the heart of their every action, and I felt a healing touch from their sincerity and grace. I could go on but, besides my lovely and amazing sister as a vessel of love, strength, and understanding, there were certainly a few others that stood by me. My sister aggressively searched for me, and this led to a reunion with my parents eventually, all fearing me dead due to my non-functional state and unreachability through these few cherished gems, whether friends or relatives, I certainly restored my faith in humanity. I was learning to heal throughout all of the chaos, yet these glimmers of light and healing touches brought me clarity and my sense of dignity with the contrast. It wasn't easy – by a few I literally mean I was a person surrounded by large crowds and social situations in what I'll now call my old life, and just one friend living an hour away and a few distant acquaintances remained in what I'll now call my new life.

This was a time when I am also learning about how people give with fresh eyes. There were crucial takeaways, and I may have never understood if I didn't have this life-altering experience. On one end, there was a profound disappointment, and on the other, there was profound hope. Seeing how people give through the eyes of someone living life in reverse or turned upside down, has changed me forever. I've decided after these experiences to always give of my heart, based on trusting my intuition, and without placing any undue pressure or interrogation on the recipient. I vow to see with the gentle and truly empathetic eyes of humanity.

When someone is an independent, self-sufficient person that has demonstrated lifelong achievement, it is extremely difficult even to ask the simplest favor. That is, at least, how it was for me. Since I was not in a state of self-love, but rather worthlessness, this was excruciatingly painful and humiliating to the degree that I can barely utter with words. Asking was hard enough, but rejection styles showed the true colors of people.

WHY IS SELF-LOVE SO IMPORTANT?

It's the puzzle all of us deal with as we work towards healing and restoring wounded self-esteem. We intend to value and love ourselves more. We certainly know the suffering when those old feelings of unimportance creep in. We even understand the areas where we're most delicate as well as self-critical.

But just how in the world do we transition from these wincing, self-negating sensations to feelings of self-love? How do we like ourselves when in many ways, we so shatteringly do not?

If you're experiencing this quandary, don't worry. In finding your journey to self-love, it will commonly appear as a roadblock. This noticeable deadlock is absolute to be expected.

And here's why: to feel love and feel that healthy and balanced feeling of self, we have first to feel complete and nourished. The issue is that these self-negating sensations stop us from being appropriately nourished and healed.

This is especially true when these harmful feelings run deeply to our feeling of self - our self-image - our very identity. Due to the fact that we largely see ourselves through this wounding-- as not nearly enough (not perfect enough, not thin enough, not achieved enough, etc.) -- we deprive ourselves of that basic, ongoing esteem-nutrition we need to experience that sense of completion.

And there's our double-edged sword. We cannot see our worthiness can be filled; and also, we cannot aid ourselves to see our merit.

The Bridge To Self-Love

Fortunately, there is an intermediate action, a setting that links the divide between that deficient state of self-rejection and also your all-natural full sense of self-love. It's a placement that helps us start to feel nurtured, despite the self-negating sensations, so we're able to revive and rekindle that natural sense of being okay and being enough.

And that intermediate setting is self-acceptance as well as self-compassion. Unlike that mystical, distant land of self-love, this intermediate placement is remarkably simple to find, and also remarkably powerful.

Self-acceptance and self-compassion are not about attempting to encourage yourself that you're lovely or successful when your wounded feelings are currently telling you that you're not. And it's definitely not concerned with exhausting yourself attempting to repair what's "incorrect" with you to ensure that you satisfy that harsh, perfectionist sight. Neither of these feedbacks does much to nurture you at a deep level.

Relocating into this intermediate placement needs absolutely nothing more than treating yourself patiently and compassionately in response to these uncomfortable feelings and excruciating minutes.

Make no mistake. You're not rejecting these injured feelings. And you're not refuting that they hurt. You're just replying to these unpleasant feelings in a different way.

Serving 'You' Instead of Your Injured Feelings

You're embracing a different position. You're taking a step back and recognizing that, as genuine as these injured sensations appear, they remain in truth simply that: wounded feelings. They are sensations being produced by a wounded area. They're not offering you precise details regarding your merit. They're just signaling you to a hurt area.

And also, in reaction to that harm area, you need most importantly to be gentle, understanding, and kind toward yourself.

Once again, note the distinction. As opposed to breaking down right into these incorrect, self-negating sensations - instead of believing them, treating yourself as a rotten individual, and also pushing yourself even harder-- you choose to treat yourself with respect, positive treatment, and with compassion. You respond to this unpleasant signal by using generosity as well as recognizing these excruciating feelings.

Keep in mind, restoring your self-confidence is not concerning "dealing with" yourself. It's about feeding yourself. Your work is not to satisfy this wounded view of yourself or your life. Your task is to resolve the injury underlying it: to nurture the deprived, evaluated location at the root of it.

You do this by treating this place, not with violence; however, with persistence and also empathy.

That crushing need and desire to repair yourself is a sign of your wounded self-esteem. This harsh method towards yourself is a repeating of the wounding, denying behavior.

So, when you choose to treat yourself comfortably as well as compassionately, you're, in fact, damaging that pattern of self-harshness. When you can step back and also begin to be personable and accepting of yourself, regardless of what you think is wrong with you, that real sense of you begins to be nourished.

It wakes up. And as you proceed with this strategy, your healthy and balanced feeling of self-expands stronger and more powerful.

And simply to be clear. Self-acceptance does not prevent you from taking favorable activity for your growth as well as improvement, or perhaps making necessary modifications in your life. These initiatives need you to be especially encouraging, kind, and gentle towards yourself. This is the very fuel you need to heal, make changes, and advance.

An RX For Those Painful Minutes of Self-Rejection

It goes without saying, but compassion and patience will most likely not be your preliminary impulse when that sensation of insignificance initially rears its ugly head. Once again, initially, we'll wish to fall right into these agonizing feelings.

So, when this takes place, we need to pull ourselves back just a little bit and keep in mind that these are not accurate feelings. These are wounded feelings routing you to an injured place. Let the discomfort advise you to be gentle and healing with yourself.

Consider it a prescription for these tough minutes. And the more responsive as well as agonizing these places are, the much more compassionate and gentler you need to be with yourself. You could additionally add a dosage of lightness to this prescription.

The challenges we deal with in learning to like ourselves is that the particularly agonizing sensations connected with injured self-esteem have the unfortunate capability to remove our sense of self as well as self-respect altogether - to make sure that, basically, we can locate no self to enjoy. We need to be ready for this very human reaction to our wounding and locate empathy for it.

Luckily, patience, as well as empathy, are acts of love. Particularly when they're guided toward yourself. And also, this tiny action will certainly start right away to bring you back to yourself: back to fullness as well as back to love.

Steps To Embrace Self Love.

Some of us leave connections for new ones similar to squirrels leaping from branch to branch. We feel turned down by the lack of love from someone, and we quickly find a replacement to maintain our very own dependence. Yet others are afraid of solitude and create distractions in their house (i.e., television, computer system, or music) to escape from the illusion of privacy.

What we lack is love for ourselves or self-love. Self-love is a deep link to our psyche, which is the resource for drawing in all things we desire, including lasting, sustainable connections.

The love for ourselves bring in deeper links with others when we find how to appreciate all things that stem from our inner growth while, in tandem, eliminating self-criticism as well as judgment.

Here are steps to promote even more self-love into your life:

Remove judgment - When you evaluate others, you are judging yourself. Offer more acceptance of others since you'll become a more forgiving and accepting person of your own mistakes too.

Verify your life - Promoting affirmations is approving the positives of what holds about you. For example, if you state you are a gifted and intelligent individual, then you are! No one can take your affirmations from you, especially if you believe they ring true. The more you attest your words, the more you believe them as your truth. The best affirmations begin with "I Am" as a statement. Locate the top positive qualities of yourself and recite them to yourself each and every day.

Clear the Mess - Try shutting off the noisy elements in your environment (i.e., TV, computer, music) and spend some time in peaceful reflection. Turning off interruptions will allow you to turn inward for your answers.

Meditate - Part of removing disruptions consists of quieting your mind. Get to an area of tranquility and satisfaction by practicing day-to-day meditations. You can find various guided reflections or practice various types of deep relaxation as well as power recovery via Yoga exercises, Reiki, and more. Sometimes the very best reflection is experienced during peace and quiet. Find time to head out in nature and sit quietly.

Desire to Inspire - We can locate the gift of inspiration in all points if we look for them. Whether you pay attention to lyrics in tune or observe the shape of fallen leaves on a tree, aspire to discover the ideas and appeal regarding life every day.

Self-love resembles a mirror, which indicates your love for others will just be as deep as you love yourself. Caring for yourself in a deep and also significant way will certainly enable you to share a love for others with much deeper meaning and also feeling. Attempt these actions to promote self-love, and witness just how the attraction of true love is returned as well as changes your life in all ways.

HOW DO YOU LOVE YOURSELF?

Step 1: Say No and Stop Overextending Yourself

One of the best ways you will love yourself more is when you learn to set limits and say "No" to overstretching yourself too much. It is easy to desire perfection that you forget to delegate, whether at home or in the office. Realize that while you seek perfection, you are depleting your energy and motivation and harming yourself spiritually, mentally, physically, and emotionally.

So many people often overextend themselves beyond what they are capable of doing. Just because you don't want to let people down does not mean that you should shoulder every task to be done. It is totally fine to say that you have enough on your plate and will not take on any more activities. Don't just agree to help everyone at the expense of your happiness.

Saying "No" does not mean that you are rude or selfish. It means that you are aware of what is best for your wellbeing and are willing to do what makes you happy first before you can think of the rest of the world.

The trick is to learn when to delegate and take the burden off your shoulders. Also, learn to protect yourself from toxic people in your life. If there are people who drain you instead of building you up, it is time you start cutting them loose. You simply do not possess all the time in the world to go around hanging out with people who drain you of your sunshine and leave you empty and sad. When you cut lose negative people from our life, you will start to love and respect your self-worth more.

Step 2: Prioritize Your Priorities

One thing you need to know and understand is that there will always be something more to do every day. What is important is to order all tasks in order of priority. Ask yourself how urgent and important a task is. Think about all the things that are most important and you have to do them to survive. Those are the things which matter the most and should be at the top of your priority list.

The least important things should be at the bottom of your list. Then you can start by doing the most important tasks at the top of your priority list. Then when you have time left, you can start doing the least important stuff.

When it comes to self-love, free time is also an important task. However, whenever you feel that you are overstretching, this time is an essential part of your calendar that you cannot ignore. If you fail to observe your free time, then what you are simply choosing is to overstretch yourself too much on things that can wait or those that do not matter anyway.

For instance, if every night you have some work to do that you carry home with you from the office, you must schedule at least one or two nights in a week that you sit home and spend that time doing the things you love most other than working. You can relax with your family, watch your favorite TV show or soak in the tub, sipping your favorite glass of wine. Trust me; you need it!

Step 3: Establish A Self-Reflection Routine

One of the best and most effective methods is to self-reflect is to practice meditation. This is one of the best ways you can focus on YOU and the present moment you are in. Well, you don't need to meditate for several hours. Even 15-30 minutes can go a long way in helping you focus on you and what matters to you most. When you spend this time focusing on nothing other than your breath is one of the best ways to feel less frazzled.

Start by identifying a peaceful place where you can sit quietly. Then set the alarm or timer for the amount of time you would like to spend focusing on you. Close your eyes and breathe. Pay attention to your breathing and allow your thoughts to appreciate everything good you have in your life. This is not the time to begin worrying about this and that. It is time for you to love yourself and appreciate all the efforts you make every day. When the timer goes off, you can get back to your work.

Another way to focus on you is by attending yoga sessions. If you can't resist the thought of just sitting alone in a quiet space, sign up for yoga sessions. Trust me; this is the ultimate way to relax and take care of yourself.

Step4: Put Your Basic Needs First With A Self-Care Routine

As girls, it is often our job to take care of everyone else. Unfortunately, we take care of everybody but ourselves. At times, you must put aside everyone else so that you can focus on meeting your basic needs first. Realize that if you are taking care of others at the expense of your emotional and mental wellbeing, then it is not worth it.

You must find the time and schedule in your routine to take care of yourself. You need time to let go of everything and everyone so that you can decompress. When you don't take the time to decompress, you will not be able to recharge, and this alone can put so much strain on you. You can choose to do anything during this time that strengthens your wellbeing. Whatever it is, dedicate yourself to doing it and watch how much strength you gain.

You will be unstoppable!

HOW TO BELIEVE IN YOURSELF?

Who Am I Really?

Have you ever asked yourself this question? If so, it is not surprising and also not abnormal. You can ask yourself who you are. Because even if you know it, the question still arises as to whether your personal view is true. The self-image is subject to many fluctuations and can be negative, but of course, also positive. To understand this process, it is important to know the reasons. A self-image, also known as self-esteem, is composed of the following conditions, among others:

For you, it is important what other people think about you: it does not pass you by without a trace, and you think about their words.

You see yourself! They perceive certain traits and may even question them.

You have gained experience in your childhood and, of course, take it with you into your future.

Your successes, but also your defeats, play an essential role in your life.

This is only a small selection of the circumstances that can shape your self-image and change it again and again. The goal is to allow the positive to happen. But often negative experiences creep in, and a positive self-image becomes a negative image. Special emphasis is placed on the words that other people say about us. But also the thoughts about ourselves can change a lot. However, the foundation for a negative self-image is often laid in childhood. Now it would be advisable to start here and not allow it to happen in the first place. But unfortunately, this is not possible!

Because as a child, we are not able to see our personality. We accept what other people tell us, in most cases, of course, our parents. If negative thoughts and words often determine everyday life, here we run the risk in the future of seeing ourselves like this!

The good thing is that you are always capable of influencing your self-image positively. Even if you get into a whirlpool of bad thoughts, it does not mean that it will stay that way forever. Believe in yourself and create a picture that suits you!

If you manage to do this and believe in yourself and your ability, your self-image will also change positively.

This step is important and, at the same time, brings you closer to further success: you can gain new self-confidence. Stand by yourself and your thoughts, and don't take on the words of your environment too much. A piece of advice is always good and can sometimes provide the decisive hint that remains hidden from you. But your own opinion should always have priority and not be seen as secondary. If you can recognize and also convert this, the love for itself and a new attitude towards life is not far away anymore.

Create Your Own Dream Image

The first step to improve your perception is your wishes! When was the last time or moment you asked yourself what you wanted? Even if thoughts fill us again and again and dreams briefly flare-up, you often drown in everyday life. There is no time to question them or perhaps even follow them more closely.

Use the time of the day that is only meant for you. Even if you say now that these hours do not exist, they will still exist. And should it not be the case: create free space for yourself! These times are essential, not only for yourself but also for your thoughts.

Now, try this: sit down and take a piece of paper and a pen. Relax for a bit, take a deep breath, exhale and try to become one with your dreams. Write down what you want and what goals you want to achieve. It does not matter whether your thoughts and ideas are attainable or not.

It is crucial to think about it and put it on paper. This alone makes them more real and makes it easier to define your possibilities. You can sort out what is important to you and what may no longer need to be fulfilled.

It is essential to have goals or wishes and to accept them. There's no wish that is not worth it! Ask yourself this question: "Who do I want to be?" and find your answer! But what if a dream doesn't come true? Then take it! This small list of your feelings and wishes is an important step to recognize yourself as a person with your goals.

No life is without happiness and joy, just because a dream remains such a dream! Because the pure existence of a person himself is the greatest gift.

Revealing Strengths And Accepting Weaknesses

In the search for ourselves, we will also meet again and again our strengths and also weaknesses that make us a person and make us unique. Often we tend only to want to see what makes us feel good about ourselves. We always want to "look good" or "look presentable" in front of other people. Especially professionally, we would rarely admit weaknesses. Too great is the fear of losing and not being good enough for the job. If you resigned, that would be the worst thing that could happen to you! And here they are again: fears, negative thoughts, and a false self-image. Strengths and weaknesses make a person. No one can do everything well and without any mistake. There must always be a negative side. The decisive factor is how we see them and how we present them to the outside world.

Do not hesitate to show your skills openly! You can do it quietly and be proud of yourself. Some truly have worked hard for it and have not achieved so much. But you may and should also accept your weaknesses. Don't push them aside, but accept them into your personal life.

But is it difficult for you to see both sides and accept certain things? No problem: Here, too, notes and pencils can help you! Sketch a table and compare your weaknesses with your strengths. You will find that there is no imbalance. Where there are weaknesses, there are strengths! Conversely, of course, it is the same.

Take your time and look at your remarks in more detail than ever before. Are your weaknesses so serious, and is it not worth talking openly about your skills? You've earned it!

Acknowledge who you really are! You are not required to be perfect at all times and be able to do everything! It is not present in the nature of man to be an ideal individual. It is much more important to see oneself and to accept oneself in all its facets.

Do not allow external images to become self-image.

Everything could be so much simpler if it weren't for this last and much too great stumbling block: the external image. It shows us what other people think about us. These opinions weigh heavily and often outweigh one's own emotions. This can be seen, for example, when you are very convinced of something.

You've got a plan. You are interested in attending a training course and exercises because it has always been your dream to continue in this direction. In your mind, you have already planned everything! Only registration is still missing.

Shortly before the decisive signature, an acquaintance joins in and raises doubts. Perhaps he sees a lack of time or even overestimation of his abilities as disruptive factors. No matter what, he "leads into the field": You are insecure and suddenly don't even know whether your idea was as good as you thought it was! You'd better give up before you get started, shouldn't you?

This situation catapults us directly into the so-called external image. Here the words and opinions about ourselves through another person are more important than one's thoughts. At certain moments, a good advice can be helpful, but sometimes it can be annoying. If you are firmly convinced of yourself and your idea, then it cannot be wrong. And if it doesn't work, you were brave and took a step that many people wouldn't have taken in the first place. You no longer have to doubt or ask yourself what would have happened if you had taken a short risk.

Self-image and external image work closely together, and self-awareness can easily be unsettled and thus also influenced. If you look at yourself now, you may even find yourself wrong! Have courage and become the person you want to be. You are not "small" and "insufficient". You have got a strong personality, and everything you have achieved to date shows your ability and strong will.

Never neglect your dreams or yourself! Create the self-image that shows you the way you are!

HOW TO BE HAPPY WITH YOURSELF

Happiness is a conscious and disciplined choice that can only be felt from within. To experience happiness, you must realize that there is no emotion to be released, no need, no condition to be met, nothing to be fulfilled. However, most of the time, you have developed the art of being unhappy; you have memorized the suffering. You are constantly complaining, feeling sorry or making excuses for yourself, or accusing others, making them responsible for how you feel. You act and react, but you never feel good; you simply do the next thing or achieve the next something, and never get satisfaction. Understand that you can be happy, despite the drama around you. Happiness is not an automatic process; it takes conscious effort. To heal is to make yourself happy. In short, you must release your unhappiness. Happiness comes and stays when you consciously change your predominant internal focus. Give up the belief that you do not deserve happiness. Act deliberately to oppose any negative or moody feelings. Just realize that you do not need them in your life for anything. When you are in a bad mood, do not obsess over it. There are always mental and physical habits linked to your negative state of mind. You are always anticipating a bad outcome or ruminating about what had happened when something went wrong. You are never in the present moment. Doing nothing to change your bad mood is not acceptance, but carelessness and a lack of emotional intelligence.

You must invite happiness in and feel it filling you up from the inside. Would you like to live peacefully and move on with your life? You can choose to have a happy feeling anytime you want. Focusing on happiness, you can create new neural networks in your brain.

To change your inner state, you must improve your breathing and posture. Learn how to have happy physiology, because correct posture attracts happy thoughts. Keep your back straight, breathe deeply from your belly, and look up with a smile on your face. Just allow good feelings to become all you are. Just say to yourself: "I accept you, I am sorry, I forgive you, please forgive me, thank you, I love you."

Be humble, responsible, forgiving, grateful, loving, be happy first, and the things you want will follow. Humility is strength and wisdom, not weakness and ignorance. Humility gives you a better perception. Also, you will find peace only by complete forgiveness. Just feel this new way of being. Insist on being it, so that nothing from the external world can disrupt you. Moreover, do not forget to stay awake; often, people feel threatened by your aliveness and try to suppress it, as their aliveness was suppressed before by others.

Your Ego tries to convince you that it can give you what you need to be complete or happy, and you believe its lies. You start to seek happiness outside yourself. You own things and attach to people or situations, but you slide more deeply into a sense of unhappiness and loneliness. The Ego's teachings are illusions, and following them will only create more suffering. The image of yourself you see through your Ego is a deprived, unloving, and weak one. You must stop seeing this distorted picture of yourself and others; you feel miserable because you cannot love this picture.

The Ego creates a feeling of emptiness that you are unable to fill, a false feeling of not being complete. Often, to fill your nothingness from within, you want to be saved by the love of a romantic partner. You try to get people to be your reflection. You might have a continuing need always to have the company of others. When your desire to be loved is just another unmet need from childhood, you spend your life seeking parents in friendly or romantic relationships. If your parents have neglected you, as an adult, you desire mature love from others, from surrogate parents. Therefore, you do not see people for who they are; you project your unresolved issues onto them. You cannot exclude yourself from what you project. You try to use others to heal your wounds that occurred in the past. You need someone to merge with, and you can waste your whole life searching. No matter whoever you have around you, you will still feel separate. When you seek happiness in relationships, and your attention and energy are focused on getting others to meet your needs, just realize that no real happiness can be obtained from others or given to another person. As long as you hang on to a sense of separate and independent self, you will suffer.

Under the pretext that "we are, by nature, social beings," the Ego encourages any behavior that satisfies "genetically encoded needs," such as love and belonging, or power and freedom. Recognize what you are trying to do. You are following Ego's teachings. To feel Ego-based love, you struggle to find a good relationship. To sense the power, you try to find someone to obey you. However, to feel free, you should get rid of precisely what you are trying to do to others, namely to control them. When you cannot give your Ego what it wants, you become unhappy.

People only pay attention when something changes. The unusual is perceived as significant, while the ordinary is almost invisible. Some people believe they need change to be happy. Even when they have everything they want, they get used to it and end up ignoring it. People can get bored until they simply do not care anymore.

Do not confuse the real happiness with temporary emotions produced by Ego-based desires. Your Ego wants to be liked, respected, or appreciated, which would give you the impression that another person makes you feel good, happy, or loves you. Everything stops or dies at a time.

The Ego cannot love, but it is engaged in the search for love, being unable to recognize it or find it. The Ego is a failure in communication anyway, no wonder it is competitive rather than loving. The Ego distorts love because it is afraid of it. Often, the Ego despises the person who is with you and longs for someone else, disliking what it has and craving for what it does not have. You must decide to manifest love, and, as you project it, you will see love both inside and out. When your project love, you will find it. You can only receive love from others and give love to anyone or everything. If you refrain from defining, labeling, or judging another person, if you are aware, grounded, and present in the moment, without needs, past, or future, you may try to share your stillness with a person like you, in a supportive and respectful relationship. To love is to give another person a supportive space, to respect his or her stillness.

CAN YOU LOVE SOMEONE IF YOU DON'T LOVE YOURSELF?

Being lovable means being worthy of love—period! There are no exemptions or exceptions.

The very fact that you exist means that you are worthy of love and therefore are lovable. To be clear, I'm not whether your behavior is always lovely. Let's face it; some of our actions stemming from our lack of self-love are not particularly lovable. However, I am not talking about behaviors or actions. I am talking about your core being—not your personality traits or behaviors that were born out of loathing. Your core being is lovable. I repeat: Your core being is lovable. There is nothing in your makeup or how you were designed that makes you unlovable to the universe.

However, for many of us, this truth has been beaten out of us, either metaphorically or literally. We begin to see our lovability as something that is negotiated: "I will find you worthy of love if you do X, Y, and Z for me." Perhaps your lovability is contingent on someone else's mood for the day; one day, you are worthy of love, and the next day that person can't stand the sight of you. Over time you begin to see your lovability as something to be bestowed onto you by outside forces, and that false notion will set you up for a lifetime of disappointment. There is nothing crazier than asking someone else who is most likely struggling with his or her issues of self-loathing to prove to you that you are lovable. It is asking the blind to lead the blind!

You are worthy of love, no matter who you are or what you have done. Just as a newborn baby is worthy of his or her mother's love, you are now and will always be worthy of the universe's love. Others' reactions to you may have impacted your belief about your lovability, but in truth, their reactions and expressions have more to do with them than you. Your worthiness of love has nothing to do with another person, nor do you need to have others confirm that worthiness. A person who lives on top of a mountain by himself can be rooted in the truth that he or she is lovable, while a person surrounded by family and friends may secretly feel unlovable. It is not about who is in your life or how many people are around you. It is about what you know inside of you.

Self-love is about the self. For many people—especially women who have been trained to find their worthiness of love in relationship to others (e.g., a good wife or good mother)—this can be a hard truth to accept. Nonetheless, it is true. Your worthiness of love must begin with the self. You cannot find your lovability through other people. It doesn't work. And the real paradox is that without your heart being rooted in the truth that you are worthy of love, you will never allow others' love for you fully into your heart.

If you can't believe in your lovability, why do you think you will believe it any better simply because it is coming from another person? And what happens to your lovability if and when that person leaves your life? I am not saying it doesn't feel good to have others make you feel worthy of love, but it is a temporary fix. And just like an addict, you will be on the constant lookout for your next fix, thus being permanently beholden to your pusher of choice. I know it is comforting to the ego to have the world see that someone believes you are lovable. But none of these outside influences will fill up the hole you feel on the inside.

You want to have the truth of your lovability locked deep within your heart, never dependent on another. That is why many relationships (romantic or friendships) are codependent, with each person looking for proof of their lovability through the other. Healthy relationships have two people, each rooted in self-love, coming together to express that love in responsible partnership.

So if you want to experience your lovability, you must look within and find out what you believe about your lovability, and what is keeping you from living this truth.

HOW TO LEARN TO LOVE YOURSELF AFTER A BREAKUP

When you initially get your heartbroken, a huge part of the pain is the false belief that no one will compare to your ex. You think about how attractive they were, how muscular he was, and how her butt was so big. You think about how well they treated you, how she cooked your meals, and how he always surprised you with date nights. You think about how good the sex was, how he knew what spots to touch, and how she always wore sexy lingerie. I get it; you miss them. But to jump this hurdle and get to the finish line, you need to retrain your brain to think differently about them. I'm sure you've heard the saying, 'perception is reality'. Keep that phrase in mind, because how you perceive your ex after the breakup will reflect the length of time it requires you to move on. I'm going to help you perceive them the right way so you can speed up this process.

Tip 1: Think about the Bad

Okay, I know this may sound crazy because you need to remain positive, but when you think of your ex, I need you to get really negative. Going through a breakup causes you to remember all the good things Jane or John did, which in turn only makes you feel bad. I'd like you to think instead about the things they did that got on your nerves. Think about the way he snored like a gorilla or the clumps of hair she left in the sink. This will allow you to stay strong when you think about contacting them or driving to their house to stand outside their window singing Sam Smith Stay with Me.

When I wanted to call my ex in the past or look at his Instagram, it was because I remembered everything about him that made me smile. To counter that, I began to think about the bad things and the reason why I left in the first place. If you can't remember the bad, then grab that letter to your ex I told you to write, and read it. You need to return to the time when you realized that you're leaving them or them leaving you was for the best.

Tip 2: Not everyone you lose is a loss

I'm sure everyone has heard the song Best Thing I Never Had by Beyoncé, but if you haven't, listen to it and let it marinate. In the song she speaks about how she wanted someone so bad at one point, he became the best thing she never had. It's kind of like that old crush you had in high school that you were crazy about, but when you saw them last month in the mall, your first thought was, "What was I thinking?!" Think about your ex that way. Of course, they have some good traits, but were those traits really meant for you? When I think about the men I've dated who were great catches, but the relationships failed, I consider that the reason it didn't work out was probably because we weren't really that compatible. When I say everyone isn't a loss, it doesn't necessarily mean that the person was bad, but possibly just that the two of you were incompatible. It would help if you embraced this freedom so you can find someone you're more compatible with. So stop perceiving your failed relationship as a loss and recognize that it was really again.

Tip 3: There is better out there

It is so hard to see the silver lining sometimes when going through a breakup…especially when you were so in love with this person you thought it was just perfect. I am here to tell you that there's no man or woman is perfect and that there will always be better. Now, when you're in a relationship, it's great when you think about your boo as irreplaceable because you love them so much, but truth be told, no one is irreplaceable. You had a great run, but it's time to pass the baton to someone else. I say this because so many people get caught up with the thought that they cannot find anyone better when this is just false. You should know and must understand that everything happens for a reason in life, and if someone leaves your life for whatever reason, it may well be because something better awaits you.

Tip 4: Rediscover the True You

One of the main reasons people tend to remain in an unhealthy relationship is because they have completely lost themselves. They forget how to function without having that person with them as if they have no identity without them. Well, this could be because you have compromised and sacrificed so much for your relationship that you simply don't even remember who you are anymore. In a healthy relationship, you know exactly who you are separate from your partner because your partner encourages you to stay true to who you are and accepts all parts of you. When you have someone who is constantly nagging you about the things you do and how you act, encouraging you to change facets of your personality, then that isn't healthy. They don't love you for you because if they did, they wouldn't ask you to change so much of who you are. True acceptance in a relationship is your partner seeing you for exactly who you are and appreciating all of it, good and bad, and not nagging you to change. Take this breakup as a sign that you need to figure out who you are again, because maybe you lost yourself, and a large component of your current pain is your inability to see who you are without them.

Tip 5: You are Worthy of More

We have all committed mistakes, and we all have flaws, but don't let that keep you stuck in an unhealthy relationship. I've seen women remain with abusive boyfriends because that man has convinced them that they have gained too much weight or they have kids now so no one will ever want them. These are all lies engineered to keep you under their control because they don't want to see you happy. There is someone for everyone, so never think that having imperfections or baggage means you have to settle for less. Men, this goes for you, too. Maybe you lost your job, or you don't have money to splurge. There is still a good woman out there ready and willing to love you for good in your heart. Don't let your insecurities keep you from believing that you don't deserve the best. We are all worthy of strong, unconditional love, so never settle for less. You are worthy of the best!

WHAT IS THE BEST WAY TO PRACTICE SELF LOVE?

All of these factors combined make up what I believe to be self-love, and if you want to learn to love yourself, you will need to learn and develop each of these components to healthy levels. Since my aim in this book is to try to teach you how to love yourself correctly, I want you to understand what you need to have to be able to love yourself completely.

Self-Esteem

In the simplest of terms, self-esteem is generally what you think of yourself. It can be said that confident people have a high degree of self-esteem while those lacking in confidence have low self-esteem. It usually develops through a combination of upbringing and personal experiences that shapes the way we view ourselves.

Most kids who grow up with loving parents initially develop a high level of self-esteem because parents would always tend to complement their child regardless of their actual abilities. It is the same with society in general. Normal adults always praise children and are generally encouraging. No reasonable person would think to give a child negative criticism.

As a result, we as children have a high level of self-esteem because most of the feedback we get is positive, and adults try to be as kind to us as they can. As we grow up, the feedback we are given becomes more honest, and our view of ourselves starts to shift into a more realistic one.

Self-Esteem is dynamic. It changes depending on a person's status and perception of themselves. During times of failure, self-esteem normally goes down because we generally also receive negative feedback while in periods of success, self-esteem goes up because the feedback we get is also positive. It is your evaluation of yourself, based on the feedback you get.

It is not always grounded in reality, and it can be subject to changes in a person's condition or social environment. It is also a result of the accumulation of the experiences and affirmations that we have had since childhood which builds an image in our minds about who and what we are and where we ideally should stand in the social order.

Self-confidence

Self-confidence generally refers to your faith in your abilities. It develops from awareness or at least a perception of what you are capable of. For example, if you believe that you are terrible at math, then your confidence in tackling mathematical problems will naturally below. If you think that you are a terrible dancer, then you would tend to avoid dancing-related activities.

Like I said earlier, it is about your faith in your abilities and is not always tied to reality. You can be confident about your singing abilities because you believe that you have a golden voice while, in reality other people who hear you sing think the opposite. Because of your misguided confidence in your singing abilities, you might be inclined to actively promote yourself as a singer regardless of what your actual voice quality is.

If you ever watch talent shows on TV, you will see a lot of people who have a high level of self-confidence in their given sets of skills and abilities. They view themselves as extremely talented and try to impress the judges and audience only to be disappointed when they do not win or even get angry if they receive a fair criticism from the judges.

It is because self-confidence does not necessarily reflect your actual abilities but instead reflects what you think of your abilities. It is similar to self-esteem in that it usually comes from your upbringing and personal experiences, but it differs from it by being more specific. You usually develop your confidence in particular abilities because of the feedback you have received whenever you display these abilities.

When I was still a kid, I used to like singing in public. I used to sing at school presentations, and I thought I had a great voice because my parents would always compliment me whenever I sang. During school presentations, the audience would clap after I sing, and of course they did, what kind of adult would tell his or her child that their voice was terrible? This made me confident about my singing abilities.

When I grew up and started hanging out with people other than my parents, I started getting feedback that was not always positive whenever I sing. Unfortunately, people become more honest in their feedback when you are no longer a child, so I lost confidence in my singing. While I still love to sing, I am no longer that confident about it that I would never sing on stage with an audience unless I were forced to do it.

Self-Acceptance

Self-Acceptance, on the other hand, is when you learn to accept yourself for what you are. It is when you forgive yourself for all your faults and failures. It is when you appreciate your individuality regardless of how others perceive you. It is close to self-love as having self-acceptance means recognizing your flaws and knowing all your negative traits but still appreciate yourself.

Unlike self-esteem and self-confidence, which are generally affected by other people's feedback, self-acceptance is something you attain despite the feedback you get. It is internal and more of a conscious choice rather than something that easily changes depending on what other people think.

When you learn to accept yourself, you do not judge yourself, and you do not compare yourself to others. It is aware that you have specific weaknesses, but you do not let the awareness of these weaknesses bring down your opinion of yourself.

It is accepting your limitations as a human being. It is recognizing that you are not perfect, you make mistakes, and you are not good at everything but still be okay with it. In other words, it is being contented with yourself.

Self-Awareness

Self-awareness is similar to self-acceptance in the sense that it is the acknowledgment of your traits. It is about recognizing the changes in your emotions as they happen and exerting a degree of control of your actions following these emotional changes. It understands how these emotions affect your thought processes and knowing how you act in response to these emotions.

Having self-awareness is also similar to self-acceptance in that it is also about having an accurate assessment of your weaknesses and limitations, but unlike self-acceptance, it is more about knowing how these weaknesses and limitations affect the world around you. It is about knowing how to control your own behavior despite your emotions instead of letting your emotions control how you behave.

It is like the idea of professionalism. You act according to how you are supposed to in order to get the job done correctly, regardless of how you feel about your boss or your coworkers. You treat your boss and your coworkers with respect despite feeling intense dislike for them because you understand that you need to cooperate with them to get the job done.

Having self-awareness means understanding that your emotional state can affect your performance and behavior. It knows how to interact with your environment and other people in a morally acceptable manner despite your emotional state. Having self-awareness means that you know how to control yourself.

Self-Respect

In simple terms, having self-respect means having pride in yourself, and as a result, you behave in such a way that upholds your sense of honor and dignity. It is sometimes easy to confuse having a high degree of self-esteem or confidence with a high level of self-respect, but unlike self-esteem, having self-respect does not mean simply having a high opinion of yourself.

It knows what you are worth. It is having reasonable standards for yourself and behaving according to those standards. You do not settle for less because you know how much your worth, and you do not hesitate to ask or demand what you deserve.

You are probably familiar with the phrase "Don't sink to their level," right? Having self-respect means exactly that. It means not compromising your standards for anyone, even if they do not have any standards. It is about valuing yourself, and because you value yourself, you do not let other people treat you any less, no matter who they are.

Having self-respect also means that you have integrity. Your standards apply regardless of the situation. You do not bend your own rules or lower your standards just because it is easier to do so in certain situations.

If you have self-respect, you do not feel the need to beg for anyone's approval because, for you, just knowing your worth is all the approval you need. Self-respect combines the elements of self-esteem, self-acceptance, and self-awareness in that you have a reasonable opinion of yourself, you are aware of your weaknesses and limitations, and you keep your actions within an acceptable moral standard.

It means knowing who and what you are and taking responsibility for your actions. It means that you feel worthy of being loved and accepted by others. It is acting with honor and dignity because you know that you deserve to be treated with respect.

It also means knowing how to properly ask for what you deserve and standing up for yourself if you are not treated with respect. You do not allow other people to give you less than what you ask for, and you do not let other people disrespect you.

As a result, having self-respect means you also treat others with the same level of respect because you know that treating other people poorly demeans you. Having self-respect also tends to make other people treat you with respect because they see that you have standards and that you behave according to your standards.

Personal Empowerment

Personal empowerment is positively taking control of your life. It is taking all the above factors to determine your worth and then using everything you know about yourself to set realistic goals and using your abilities to achieve them. It is knowing your weaknesses and aiming to improve on them, and it is knowing your strengths and using them to advance yourself.

Having personal empowerment means knowing how to take control of your circumstances to achieve your personal goals. It is also about understanding your strengths and weaknesses well, making you better equipped in dealing with any problems that you encounter. You know how to recognize opportunities and know how to take advantage of them appropriately to succeed.

It does not simply mean having the power to make things happen. It also means knowing how to set realistic goals and having the freedom and the ability to make conscious decisions and taking the appropriate actions to achieve these goals.

ANALYZING WHAT YOU LOVE ABOUT YOURSELF

If you find the aforementioned exercises challenging and need more direction as to what your state of self-love is and where you need to develop, this guide can help you. Reflect on the person you are, as well as the person you are not. Try and think of who you are with disregard to your earlier life, the people in your life, or your present situation. Consider who you are when these elements are removed. If you find this difficult, you must keep trying until you are able to figure it out. If you end up discovering that you have a habit of identifying yourself according to any of those previously mentioned factors, then those are the areas that you need to focus on changing. Then, consider what brings you joy and what factors in your life are significant to you. A characteristic of loving yourself is able to not only know what your wishes and principles are but also to indulge in and fulfill them. If you can identify these elements in your life but realize that you have up until this point has been postponing or completely neglecting them, this will become an obvious area in which change is needed. Think about how you handle your own feelings; do you directly confront them within yourself, or do you attempt to push them away or mute them? A large factor of self-love is honest with and aware of yourself. If you can't recognize and admit your emotions, you are not honest with yourself, and this is something that is necessary in order to move forward.

You can also try and figure out your true self by examining your behaviors. You can find this particularly useful if you notice that you have a habit of doing reckless or thoughtless actions. When you recognize yourself doing these things, think about them and consider how these actions reflect you as a person, including your attitude and state of mind. If you have a slip-up, you can use this guide to recognize what exactly caused you to make an error. Additionally, when working on gathering comprehensive insight of who your true self is and is not, it is very important and recommended to make sure that this realization comes from you alone, without the influence of others' opinions. There will inevitably be many people who are accusatory and think that they have a definition of what or who you are or are not capable of, and may even think that they highly know you better than you know yourself; nevertheless, this is certainly not true. These kinds of people may not always aggressively express these thoughts about you (they could even appear to be meaning well by it), such as if they say it in the shape or form of advice rather than as a direct accusation. However, regardless of how they express these kinds of thoughts about you, these comments are most often not meant to be helpful to you. It is possible to receive constructive, fair, and unprejudiced criticism, as well as counsel and suggestions for improvement from people who are close to us and whom we trust. If you feel that this is not the case, always make sure never to let someone else's thoughts or opinions about you influence how you think or feel about yourself. No one knows you better than you do, and keeping this in mind is one of the most important things that will progress you towards loving yourself.

HOW TO KNOW IF YOU ARE FORCING YOURSELF TO LOVE

There's no way another person can "give you love." It is simply impossible.

Whenever you "fell in love," it was not because the other person was doing something magical. Love is not something that another passes on to you in a blue Tiffany box. It is just that that person meets a finite number of requirements that you conditioned yourself to believe are necessary to the experience of unconditional love. They are permissions slips that allow the love you already are to show up, in a muted form finally.

Some people are prolific about all the conditions that need to be met to experience even a tiny bit of unconditional love. Others have so many that they make it literally impossible ever to gain that permission. This is often just a coping or defensive mechanism—a way of building a "fortress" around themselves to make it impossible for love to come into their lives while PRETENDING that they want nothing but to be loved.

We are living in an endless stream of conditions that need to be met to permit ourselves to be the love we already are again. When we want to experience the flow of love through external outsourcing, then we set conditions like, "I first have to look like this" or "I have to achieve that." If we finally do achieve it, we only allow ourselves to let a little bit of love flow for a very short period of time. So, our desire for unconditional love is constantly faced with endless conditions. How about dropping all that conditioning, and going to the source of the love we already are directly instead? How about an unconditional ALLOWANCE? How about surrender? Wouldn't that be a faster and more direct path?

Let's get back to the fact that "falling in love" is not that somebody is GIVING you something (love). There is no magical "love spray" that the other person splashes on you, and you all of a sudden HAVE love. NO!

That love already IS within you. Yes, that other person can certainly inspire you or become that permission slip to love for you, especially if that person is more aligned to the love he/she already is than you are. Other people or objects or places in our lives do have their meaning and can help us to experience the love we already are. But this doesn't happen because THEY are doing something special.

It is, again, only about YOU.

It's about YOUR intent and decision to stop outsourcing love, putting it OUT THERE, and to begin purifying yourself from all that highly conditioned behavior. It's about ending the game you have been playing all this time—pretending you do NOT love and waiting for the "right person" or the "right time" to be it again.

Wouldn't it be more productive to ditch the conditions and give yourself FULL permission to be the love you already are, truly UNCONDITIONALLY? That means you accept love from yourself at any time, without any circumstance, object, person, place, or any other condition. What terrible thing has love done to you that makes you throw obstacles in its way? And more importantly, what is the benefit of this game? From my understanding: NONE!

So, let me repeat it:

There is no way another person can give you love.

I know it takes a big mental shift to digest this. It may take some time. And that doesn't mean you have to stop eating or having relationships or delivering babies or going to the places that represent any form of love for you! Not at all. But, if you keep seeing and looking for the source of the love you already are OUT THERE, then you can never really experience it fully. You will always be dependent on that external object, which will only limit your experience of the love you already are. This will place many more limits on your life.

Stop OUTSOURCING those permission slips, and start insourcing love.

Stop outsourcing those permission slips, and start insourcing love.

That means, stop looking for conditions to be met to let the love from within you flow, and start giving yourself unconditional permission every single day. This takes practice and purification of all the crap and harmful conditioning that was preventing your happiness.

Little by little, you'll gain awareness and the realization that love always flows ONLY from within you, from your own space. Then you'll be able to practice living in love and giving love more than ever. Because you ARE already love.

You ARE already beautiful.

You ARE already light.

You ARE absolute perfection.

You always have been it.

Be still within your heart now, and feel how true that is. If you still cannot feel it, at least intuitively, then increase your conviction of it. Believe that it is there. Have some faith in yourself. For too long, you were just pretending not to be love. So, starting now, permit yourself to be it again, without any conditions.

Every day, build a stronger conviction that you are nothing but love. No bubbles. No conditions. Just allowance opened heart, and surrender.

FIGURE OUT WHAT YOU LOVE TO DO

One of the biggest secrets to living a life filled with an abundance of any kind is that we need to be specific. We need to ask the universe for exactly what we want. Unless we do, it can't deliver us anything. By now, you would have had to seriously consider your belief system and exactly how the things you believe about yourself, your circumstances, your financial situation, your relationships, your career, etc. have either worked for you or against you. You may have had to change some of your thought processes and thinking habits quite drastically for these limiting beliefs to be altered in any way.

The universe operates on a number of frequencies and vibrations that we cannot see or feel. Whether we understand it or not, this is true. It is these frequencies and vibrations that we use to attract whatever happens to us into our lives. This is quite intense when you think about it because once you understand how much power you have to change your current situation, you will find that your life can be changed just as quickly. When you hear the word 'abundance', I am almost certain that the first thing that is going to pop into your mind will be money. Am I right?

Well, that's not surprising at all because money is just another form of energy... so this is where it gets truly exciting in being able to define what you want from the universe clearly! If the universe operates on frequencies and vibrations, and money is just another form of energy, it does not stand to reason that if you can tap into this frequency or energy field, you really can attract anything that you want.

This is where one of the biggest obstacles in being abundant and living the life of your dreams comes in—our frequency, vibrations, and energy is all out of sync with the universe. We are so focused on unnecessary things that we don't want that the universe is forced to deliver more and more and more of exactly the same.

Like a vicious cycle of stuff that we don't want, the only way for this cycle can be broken when we do something about it. We need to step in and make the change physically. If you constantly focus on what you don't have, you will never have anything. If you focus on being lonely all the time, guess what? You are going to spend most of your time having to deal with your own company.

We are going to look at identifying what you want and what you don't want, and then being able to project this back to the universe in such a way that all your desires are fulfilled.

Be Clear About What You Don't Want

If you are sick and tired of experiencing the same old things out of life that you are experiencing at the moment and want to attract abundance instead, the time to start is now! For the universe to give you everything that you want, you need to make a conscious decision about all the things that you don't want without really focusing on them. To achieve this can be hard because maybe for the first time in your life, you will need to sit down and analyze your life for what it is right now. You may need to face some harsh truths about what you believe about your current reality (which is something that you create, by the way). You see, until you get to the point of saying to yourself that enough is enough and that you either need or want to make some changes in your life, nothing is going to change. The good news is that we are capable of changing our lives drastically simply by changing our thought processes.

Too often, we stay where we are because we are too scared to make a move or decide to change our destiny. Remember that I have already said that doubt or fear cannot exist in the same place as faith and belief. Unfortunately, in this situation, negativity will almost always win, hands down every time! Fear is what really prevents u from receiving the blessings of abundance in our lives. It stops and slows us down from progressing and moving forward, even if the movement is ever so slight. The point is that we must decide whether we are happy with the life that we are currently experiencing.

Remember that we spoke about the countless number of thought processes that go through your head daily? Well, this is part of the solution to be clear about what you don't want in your life anymore. Each of these thoughts needs to be followed through on some or other level. We can choose how we respond to the thought that is presented to our brains. We can do this by practicing the mindfulness techniques and trying to become fully present at the moment, rather than being stuck in the past, or trying to project ourselves into the future just yet.

Some of these decisions are micro-decisions that you don't even need to think about because you have already been conditioned how to respond. An example of this would be switching off a hot tap if the water temperature was scalding; it's an automatic response. Becoming more aware of the bigger decisions that you face every day—almost all of these decisions are linked to our emotions or our feelings, and it is our emotions and feelings that the universe picks up. When we are feeling down and out, despondent and fearful, depressed and sad, guess what, this is exactly what the universe picks up on and responds by delivering to us more of the same. With our freedom to choose, though, we can try to decide to focus on those things that will lift and elevate our mood to one of peace, joy, harmony, and happiness, or even love. These vibrations and energy levels are ones that are in keeping with the laws of the universe and ones that the universe responds to better.

Once you have made the decision or choice about what you are no longer prepared to settle for in your life, it becomes easier to focus your energy toward changing your thoughts toward attracting those things that you want instead.

Be Clear With Your Desires

Napoleon Hill gave the world one of the greatest pieces of advice about attracting abundance in his bestselling book Think and Grow Rich (1937), when he said,

"Whatever the mind can conceive and believe, it can achieve". ~

Napoleon Hill

I just love the words that he uses in this simple quote because this sums up everything that you need to do for you to manifest anything successful y. It all starts with your freedom to choose what it is that you would like from the universe. The one unique and divine gift that we have each been blessed with is the power to choose. We have the power to choose exactly what we want from the universe. We have the power to choose how we feel, how we act, how we respond to certain situations in our lives. Every negative situation that we experience can be altered into a positive one through the power of choice.

The most important thing when choosing what you want is for you to be as clear as possible. The universe cannot deliver on a vague request. If you decide that you want or desire a new car, you need to be precise and specific about exactly what car you want do you want a brand-new sports car with an automatic transmission and low-profile tires? Must it have leather seats and other luxurious features? If so, what luxury features would you like it to have? What color would you want it to be? How is it going to make you feel when you are sitting behind the wheel or driving out on the open road? Can you see the difference between the two messages that you would send out to the universe? The first is vague and uninteresting, leaving a lot of room for interpretation and misunderstanding, while the second is accurate and detailed. The second version is one that paints a clear picture of exactly what you would like to experience. It gives the universe the vibration that you have already received this and are currently experiencing joy as a result. It produces a feeling and an emotion of some kind that the universe is able to work with. Once you have been able to project this request in such a detailed manner, it suddenly becomes easier for it to manifest in your life.

The same is true of wishing that you had more money. The universe doesn't know how much money you would like—you must be able to see the actual numbers, feel the emotions of how content you feel will knowing that you have complete financial freedom and that you can provide for your family. It would help if you felt all your negative emotions of the past disappearing as the chains of debt have been broken. Are you wishing for a once-off lump sum windfall like winning the lottery, or would you prefer a better source of financial security in the form of a better paying job? Maybe you would like to retire early and would like to be able to cushion your investments with some extra cash before you do. Or possibly, you want to find ways to create additional revenue streams that can supplement your current lifestyle. If this is what you want, what will these income streams look like, and how do you plan on seeing them manifest? How are you going to feel once the universe has granted these wishes?

A word of caution when you want the universe to grant you a financial wish… make sure that you focus on wealth versus need. When you focus on needing more money, that is exactly what you are going to get, if you focus on getting out of debt, all the universe hears and understands is the word "debt." You need to shift your focus on wealth and an abundance of money when you do, that's what you will enjoy!

Of course, new cars and financial freedom are only some of the things that you may desire from the universe, but they are not the only things. These are materialistic comforts that can make our lives more comfortable, sure, but there are many other things that I have mentioned like love and stronger relationships, better careers, a comfortable home, loving families, maybe it is the freedom to travel to faraway places whenever you choose.

You may desire physical health and healing. I am here and openly tell you that whatever it is that you deeply desire and ask the universe for, connected to the emotion of how you will feel if you have received it, will be manifest in your life.

HOW TO KNOW IF YOU ARE FORCING YOURSELF TO LOVE SOMEONE

We attach ourselves to our past because we have mistaken it for our identity.

We often see who we are as what we have done or what we have missed doing. What we have been able to accomplish or not. We see an image of ourselves that our mind has created and then hate it, attack it, despise it within ourselves. Then we present it to others in the nicest way for it to be loved and accepted. If it's then loved and validated from an external source, we hope to feel finally loved, relaxed, and free of fear.

You might not agree with this, but we are loved by others more often than not. Most people are seeking affection by pleasing others. Trust me, being loved and accepted by others can be pretty easy. Yet, we still don't feel truly loved. We still feel no satisfaction deep in our soul, and we hunger for more. Then, we believe we need more acceptance. So we start disclosing more about our story, our path, what we have done, what we want to do. We do this to elicit more acceptance and relevance in other people's eyes. Then again, we enjoy their praise like the most delicious dessert. This pleasure dissipates soon after and leaves us again in a state of desperation.

This desperation, if you have felt it before, is not desperation that makes you cry long and hard. It's desperation in disguise. It often makes its entrance as feelings of wanting to connect and deeply love and feel loved by someone else. Someone who doesn't know the side of us we so much despise.

Often, in this situation, people find the urge to start anew. Start from scratch. Go somewhere where no one knows them, where they can erase their past. If you are trying to erase your behavior so you do not have to look at it again, please give up on feeling loved by others for the rest of your life. You will not allow yourself the pleasure of receiving that gift, for they don't know who they are with, or so you think. Even if they love you for who you are and not what you have done, you do not love yourself in the same way. How can we then feel loved if we don't fully love ourselves?

Words of Wisdom

Easier said than done. Most of us oscillate between wanting to be open and truthful and wanting to hide just this little piece that is, after all, oh-so-irrelevant.

Until you are receiving the most wanted hug from someone you care about, and then a shameful thought about yourself enters your head. Between the fight of your mind and your heart to decide if you are worthy of the hug, the moment is over. You oscillated between the past and future at such a high frequency you fell astray from the present.

The same way we sometimes come clean with someone else, we should come clean with ourselves. In such a way that makes us see and understand the struggle the other part of us is experiencing on a daily basis.

Do not despise that other person inside and judge it like you judge others! Someone said: The way you judge others is the same way you will be judged. We do not have to go too far to find someone who would judge us that way. It is ourselves. And as a matter of fact, that's why we judge others in the first place. Because that is the way, we treat ourselves.

I wonder then if we judge others harshly because we do the same to ourselves. Can we love others if we do not fully love and accept ourselves?

We have heard so many phrases like, love yourself before you love others in so many ways, shapes, and shades. But how do we do that? It's not a button we have hidden somewhere that we can push that will naturally awaken a dormant part of us. It is not as simple as executing a command, and voila, we suddenly love ourselves.

It's not a button, but wait, could it be?

A button is a trigger that kicks off one or a series of commands to be executed. In the case of self-love, the button is the decision you make, and it's the trigger, the desire, and the belief you need to love yourself. This puts in motion the commands to achieve what you want.

But wait, how many times have we flipped that switch? How many times have we pressed that button? Tomorrow I start loving myself. Or wait, I love myself now. Yet it hasn't worked.

You still expect. You still expect others to accept you so you can truly love yourself. And I'm talking about higher love here.

I mean loving yourself at such a degree, deeply and profoundly, that you can love others from your true identity. Not the shade your identity has created, guided by your mind. I'm talking a love from which you can share with others your identity guided by your heart.

So, we have been pressing that button, the self-love-now button, and nothing comes out. Nothing new happens. Empty. Zero. It says self-love-now, seems right. But what is going on? I press this button, and I'm just doing more of the same!

What if we are pressing the right button but in the wrong place? What if we have been hitting the self-love button from the mind and not the heart? Wait, could it be that the self-love button from the heart might yield different instructions?

Wow, I didn't know about this heart-mind thing. This is fascinating! You mean to tell me if I hit the self-love button from the heart, I will find the real instructions that would allow me to love and accept myself fully?

Well, yes. That is what I'm suggesting you do. Stop hitting the mind and asking it to do things it doesn't know how to do. This love thing is not a trade, and it's not a measurable scientific thing we can quantify, plan, or ration. The ways of the mind won't work for the things outside of its domain. And love; it is certainly from the heart.

So, what will happen if we decide to press the self-love button from the heart? First thing, the mind freaks out, like yours might be doing right at this second. It identifies all of these well-justified reasons why that's a bad idea. And why? Well, see, the mind is not only currently in control of your self-love, but of so many other things. You will find the mind is responsible for so much other heart stuff. If we could find those other things and return them to their true owner, we would experience a sense of relaxation and balance.

The real you is there is an amazing human being and a divine soul. There is nothing wrong with you, or me, I discovered. We are perfectly created; we just have a few glitches to tune-up. There are a few responsibilities that need to be reassigned, a few rules to re-write, and that's all.

Think about it, and we are so lucky that's the case. Animals and simple-minded humans live happily for the most part, but they do not fully know they are happy. They are not aware of the blessing of the journey to happiness.

But the mind freaks. That's what it does, and it does it well. That's its job, after all. The mind was created for survival, for reactive instincts. Do you know why it feels threatened when it comes to things of the heart?

Because of the mind, the heart's algorithm to love is not reliable. The mind is guided by a set of ideas and rules it believes will take us to a safe place where we can avoid pain.

The Mind Strives For Security, Not Fulfillment.

This primitive system of the mind was installed on purpose. It's okay if the mind freaks. Watch it freak. Become aware and stand in your duality. The mind sees imminent death because if you take away one of the things it controls, it messes up the rules for all else. Imagine that! If you take away love from the mind, what would happen to happiness? The mind also has a few rules for happiness that are messing you up, preventing you from reaching the top of the very feeling it controls.

You will never be able to turn off the mind's fear of death. It will always be present in your physical reality. And you can't live your daily life in an alpha-state either. So, what's left?

We are dealing with it.

Let's make peace with that first. After all, perfection is so boring! It would mean someone would love you for being perfect and not for who you are. Acknowledging your human mind, making mistakes, makes us feel the love in a whole new way. We are not perfect, yet we are loved. So embrace your imperfection, your human mind, and let's deal with it.

What's the biggest fear of the mind?

The mind's biggest fear is that if you rearrange the way it's been wired to find love and worthiness, it will mess up the algorithm, and it will never get it.

The mind thinks that pushing through with the current algorithm will lead to love someday. Do you see it? That's why, in the first place, we can't get rid of our minds.

The mind is working for the same purpose as the heart. That purpose is love.

Yet, the mind and the heart arrive at love through different means. You hear many people say when referring to a harsh person: He or she doesn't have a heart. And what do they mean? Obviously, the person does have a literal heart, or he wouldn't be walking down the sidewalk. Instead, they mean: Look, that person is not behaving from his or her heart. That person is trying to achieve a loving purpose through not-loving means. Ah! And why? Why would a loving person attempt to emotionally or physically hurt another human being in the name of love?

I know this might be a delicate question. Many of you reading this might believe you are or have been a victim of abuse. For the purpose of the self-love topic we are discussing, I want to say that a human will often react from their survival instinct when it fears death.

To that person trying to receive or feel love, it's a matter of life and death. They do not know any other means of obtaining the love they crave, and when those means are shut down, there is no way out for them. At that instant, it's either you or their survival, for they will die if they cannot experience the feeling they are so desperately seeking.

They are unable to generate such love for themselves. They are on the lookout for the person who will take responsibility for their emotions and will give them unconditional love.

This might give you a hint of why, if this is your case, you have attracted people who lack self-love to your life. You probably do not love yourself either. You are probably also looking for your love to be satisfied and validated first from an external source. You are waiting for someone to label you as lovable, so then you can relax, accept, and love yourself.

HOW TO ACCEPT YOURSELF

Seeing Past What Should Be

I would like to remind us that self-acceptance requires total ownership of our present condition.

When we look at life as something it should be, rather than what it is at the moment, feelings of inadequacy, self-doubt, and self-hatred arise. It becomes virtually impossible to accept ourselves a hundred percent when we come from a state of inadequacy and deprivation.

When we evaluate life against a preconceived model, it is easy to underappreciate the good things about our current situation.

The state of "should be" is the opposite of living with gratitude.

Self-acceptance empowers us to be in charge of our destiny. It allows us to see and enjoy all that is around us. When we incorporate self-acceptance in our lives, we move from focusing on the inadequacies of life to the abundance it offers us.

Self-acceptance is a shift from negativity towards positivity. From what should be to what is. From victimhood to gratitude. From intolerance to acceptance. From "I am not enough" to "I am enough." From impatience to patience. Self-acceptance is a door to the hidden dimension within us.

The Role Of Self-Acceptance In Relationships

To illustrate my point, let's look at why relationships fail.

Most relationships do not work because relationships are seen as something we need to make us whole.

This expectation of a relationship to make us whole is often seen in our culture and our language.

While "other half" or "better half" are common synonyms for significant others.

"Happily ever after" is emphasized and glorified as symbolizing the fact that a ring and a promise is the end goal of a relationship.

In actuality, a relationship cannot thrive if even one of the persons in the relationship is "half." "Happily ever after" is a grandiose myth romanticized historically by romantic fairy tales, and in the last century by Disney's motion pictures.

I like to see relationships in the context of cups. Each of us has a relationship cup. A full cup symbolizes serenity of mind and an ability to give to and receive from others unconditionally, as one can fulfill their wants and needs without needing anyone else to do so for them.

An empty cup symbolizes unresolved wounds from the past: an inability to give and receive love from others, marked by guilt and shame surrounding one's desires and needs. An empty cup is the epitome of the lack of self-love.

When we have an unfulfilled cup, and we do not actively fill it with acts of self-acceptance and self-love, we try to load it via unhealthy means, such as internalized anger and addictive behavior.

When we enter a relationship with a cup that is not full to its brim, one of the two things result.

Two people with empty cups end up trying to take from each other.

OR

One person with a full cup gives to the other while draining themselves.

As you may have already guessed, these conditions ensure that neither of the cups ends up full, which causes constant friction in a relationship.

It's our responsibility to fill our cup to the brim before we commit to relationship opportunities.

Why Do Communications Fail In Some Relationships?

It has been touted since time immemorial that communication is key to relationships. But we all know that communication often goes awry, and in many cases exacerbates situations that are already on the verge of explosion.

To continue with our "cup" analogy, an attempt to communicate fails because the noise resulting in the two empty cups coming together drowns out the discussion and amplifies the hurt experienced instead of healing the situation.

The principal reason for this failure is a lack of self-acceptance and the unawareness of what our exact needs are at the time of communication.

When one or all parties involved in a relationship have an empty cup—when there is a lack of self-love or self-acceptance—it becomes impossible for desires, needs, and expectations to be laid out on the table exactly as intended.

Guilt, shame about our desires, and an underlying fear of losing our partner make manipulation, deceit, and expectations of having our "mind read" a common theme in relationships.

Each person talks about why their expectations were not met in a relationship, but both parties fail to have a conversation around what these expectations were, to begin with. Communication is initiated and often ends based on the assumption one makes about the other's intentions.

People who enter into a relationship with an empty cup manage to amplify any discord and ensure that they neither understand nor are able to be understood by their partners, even though their attempts to communicate may be a genuine attempt to make the relationship work.

Why Do Others Succeed In Others?

Contrast this with two individuals who go into a relationship with their cups full. These are individuals who love and accept themselves and are in a relationship to give and receive love.

These individuals are content in themselves, and as a result, are comfortable in asking for what they want. These individuals respect themselves, their partners, and their relationship. They are committed to making the link work. They communicate to minimize the tension the inevitably arise in relationships, and they work on resolving any issues as quickly as possible.

Even with two full cups, a relationship requires work. It is a constant fulfillment of commitments, acceptance of each other's quirks, and making sure that no vague, unaddressed assumptions fester in the relationship for long.

The reason this seems effective is that when two people who are entirely content with themselves engage in giving and receiving, any resulting friction is not enough to unhinge the relationship.

As one develops the tools necessary to love and accept oneself, and in turn, is better tuned to the wants and needs of other people, one starts to let go of the shame and guilt of having desires. This also allows an individual to express themselves fully without resorting to manipulative, deceitful, "read my mind" communication tactics.

SELF-LOVE AND SELF-ACCEPTANCE

It would help if you realized by this point that the practice of self-acceptance and self-love is a lifelong endeavor. You can reach a level of self-acceptance and self-love that feels right, and you can take pride in the knowledge that you have achieved this level of success, but do not become complacent in this spot.

The road is long. It never ends. The end goal is not a destination but is simply an extension of the road. It just gets easier the longer you travel it. You are a work in progress, forging the path as you travel it, placing one brick after another in front of you, making a new place for your foot to fall.

In essence, three key elements make up your journey. We will break down the larger elements of the journey: self-acceptance, self-love, and what has emerged as the overarching goal of the journey, happiness.

Self-Acceptance

The ultimate goal of self-acceptance is to understand who you are in every aspect intrinsically and to accept yourself without recrimination or judgment.

To accept yourself is to be satisfied with yourself in every way possible. To truly understand yourself, you need to be fully aware of who you are. Your view of yourself will be understandable, as you are viewing yourself through your own eyes (though that is the only lens available to you). No one else's opinion of you matters as much as your own. How you view, yourself is vital. That you like yourself is essential.

When you are self-accepting, you see all of your strengths and weaknesses, and you accept them as parts of you. You are the collection of thoughts, emotions, and physical traits that come together to define you. Mind, body, and soul, you define yourself.

To self-accept is to let go of everything that held you back from taking control of your life and move forward. You are free of shame and guilt, past limitations, and learned behaviors. Self-acceptance has given you forgiveness for the mistakes you made along the way and the ones that you will continue to make as you move forward. It means you have overcome the limitations that your upbringing placed on you, whether it be bad parenting or a lower-income environment.

Self-acceptance is self-validation. Self-validation is greater than validation from gaining value from other people's opinions of you. You have grown beyond the need to find approval and acceptance from external sources, such as your parents, friends, or boss.

Self-acceptance is not the same as self-improvement. In order to improve something is to make it better - to fix it. To repair something is to take elements of the thing being fixed and use them to finish the product. Self-acceptance is not about making you a better person or fixing you. You cannot take pieces of yourself and rearrange them. You are not broken; you are just in a different state. Self-acceptance is about discovering who you are and why you are the way you are and then embracing it. It is an affirmation of yourself, not a re-engineering of yourself.

Nor is self-acceptance the same as self-esteem. Self-esteem values only the good qualities you find within yourself, leaving the negative out of the conversation. Self-esteem focuses only on the positive aspects of who we are. With it, we appreciate only the positive qualities we find, leaving all the rest behind.

Self-acceptance embraces every aspect of our character. It simply does not pick and select what to hold up to the light and what to leave in the shadows. It shines a light on everything, holding it all up for the world to see, including the good, the bad, and the dark.

We all have a dark side - the place where we hide the scars and bury the hurt. Some refer to it as Pandora's Box, the deep well of dark secrets that haunt us - every ill-intended thought we ever had about ourselves and the world around us but never acted upon. No light can shine there, or so you would think. But the light of self-acceptance does. It has to, as self-acceptance is universal and all-encompassing. To value yourself and to embrace every facet of who you are, you must come to terms and accept that this deep dark place plays a role in creating who you are, and you need to accept it as well.

If you understand this, you can realize what it truly means to achieve self-acceptance.

Self-Love

Self-love is a little harder to define than self-acceptance. It is not about having a big ego, and it is not narcissism, being in love with yourself, or the way you look as you catch a glimpse of yourself in every reflective surface you walk past. Self-love is not rooted in physical love nor moments of instant gratification. Buying yourself a new pair of shoes or the latest gadget on the market can make you feel good at the moment and for a little while afterward, but the feeling will fade and be replaced with the desire to consume again. Instant gratification is about to want and sometimes need, but rarely love.

To achieve self-love is to hold within yourself high regard for your well-being and happiness. Similar to what we said about self-acceptance, self-love is not the same as self-esteem. The whole self-esteem embraces and showcases the positive aspects of yourself, but when you practice self-love, you need to love more than just the good you find within. Self-love is about creating compassion for every aspect of yourself - the negative as well as the positive. It is to see yourself sympathetically and to believe you are worthy and deserving of your own love, no matter how you are portrayed.

Self-love is all-encompassing, going far beyond the mental and physical to incorporate the spiritual. It is a journey about understanding what you, at your core, need to be happy and fulfilling it. As with self-acceptance, self-love involves accepting and loving every aspect of who you are, including your weaknesses and your strengths. When you practice self-love, you are taking care of all your needs just as you would a loved one's. To do so, you need to count yourself among those you love. You are loved by yourself without question or judgment.

The sacrifices you make are for yourself, and you are willing to make them because you truly care and want to be kind to yourself. If you can incorporate the needs of others when satisfying your own, this is all the better. However, through self-love, you do not sacrifice your own personal well-being for the sake of others.

REASONS FOR LOW SELF-LOVE AND SELF-ESTEEM

Self-love and self-esteem are all about how you feel about yourself and how you judge your value. This assessment profoundly affects the decisions you make since it decides, by and large, what you view yourself as proficient and deserving of doing. When we love ourselves, we will do important things, making us progressively significant to ourselves. Without an appropriate measure of self-esteem, we do not seek after essential exercises. Instead, we stall out in a pattern of de-esteeming ourselves and not doing anything necessary to help our feeling of self-esteem.

Women with low self-esteem — who feel inadequately about themselves and judge themselves to be second-rated as compared to other people — are in danger, at that point, of not satisfying their actual potential throughout everyday life. They may not step up. They may not invest any energy into their training or professions. They may receive helpless treatment from family, companions, and sentimental accomplices. To better understand how it works, we need to look at what causes low self-esteem in people. We will discuss those causes and figure out how to fix them.

Here are a few contemplations and practices regular in individuals with low confidence and self-esteem. It tends to be valuable to recognize which ones impact you, knowing as much as possible about this is significant because once we distinguish it, we can find a way to improve it.

- They always try to evade. Maintaining a strategic distance from specific circumstances or individuals is one of the signs of people having low self-esteem and love. Such practices regularly originate from the conviction it is better to avoid and evade. Individuals that show these signs may do this to forestall pessimistic contemplations and emotions about themselves being affirmed by occasions, circumstances, or individuals.

- They attempt to satisfy others constantly, taking a stab at all that you do, trying to be 100% in control constantly, extreme seriousness. This behavior is unreasonable, and the result is unachievable, which can leave you feeling futile.

- They cover up their genuine self from others here and there, for example, their appearance, convictions, different preferences, qualities, shortcomings, and capacities. They may accept that by concealing their genuine self, they will please others, fit in well, and make themselves extremely loveable.

- They abstain from offering their input or communicating their emotions. Individuals who carry on along these lines frequently accept that they are less significant or worthy than others. They question themselves, and their capacities and accept that others are better somehow.

- They continuously look for consolation and praise from others. They think others can cause them to feel better about themselves. They always look for compassion from others.

- They want others to get things done for them because they think they are not capable enough.

- They act in a forceful manner, for example, putting others down and yelling. They reprimand others for the negative way they feel about themselves.

- They feel protective when others give them useful analysis or criticism. Since they cannot adapt to the idea that others negatively see them.

When we notice these behaviors and how these can impact us, we can begin watching out for them as we approach our everyday lives, and spot when we are acting in a manner due to our low self-esteem and harsh behavior towards ourselves. When we see how we are carrying on and why we can start testing those considerations and practices.

Consequences of Having Low Self-love and Self-esteem

To move forward in life, one needs to address the issues that hold you back. To do that, we need to see what those issues can do to us, how they impact our lives. When we know about the consequences, when we truly understand what they are, we will only be able to eliminate them or fix them. Let's see what having a lack of self-love and self-esteem can do to a person:

Depression and Anxiety

Respecting who you are at its most prominent potential is about acknowledgment. Nonetheless, living in a universe of maintaining a strategic distance from yourself, interruption from your identity, and correlation does not just keep you from closeness with yourself. However, it might even drive you further away from the individual you truly need to turn into. When we dodge acknowledgment of who we are, including our battles, a hole occurs for us inside. When we are persistently unconscious of that hole, we can without much of a stretch stall out in the dinky waters of sadness and uneasiness. Acknowledgment is respecting who you are, deep, living inside your respectability, and inside your ethical compass. In particular, it does not come without exertion. When we do not do that, it will ultimately lead to depression and anxiety.

Search for Unrealistic and Perfect Relationships

You will continually ache for more profound, increasingly valid relationships. A lot of us are great at making pseudo-associations with others. We are extraordinary at posting via web-based networking media and permitting others to see the trimmed, altered forms of ourselves. That is sufficiently not fuel for an enduring, associated boat, and it will just take us up until now. You start to look for perfect relationships, which is an unrealistic goal in the real world.

Inability to Express your Love and Feelings

At first, you are afraid to express your feelings and emotions to others. You are afraid of telling people how much you care about them. After some time, this becomes part of your personality, and you find yourself at a place where you face an extreme inability to express yourself. How would we believe and love others and fulfill their expectations, when we cannot have confidence in ourselves? There is an absence of self-esteem, there's also a suspicion of being unlovable, not at the surface, however deeply. Questioning others' affection for us fits waiting to scrutinize the profundity and truth of others' adoration.

Constant Feeling of Unworthiness

It is like you never feel you are adequate. Not adoring yourself will loan you to steady self-uncertainty, and vulnerability. Regardless of whether you are acceptable enough or not, you start to feel you are not. The more you escape from respecting you, the stronger those may turn into. Nobody can withstand long-lasting negative emotions without burnout. Consistent addressing of you, your self-esteem, and your endowments is a noisy sign to check-in and start offering self-sympathy and thoughtfulness beginning with yourself. Bless yourself with the words and pardoning, and you are anxious to provide others with.

Identifying Common Causes of Low Self-love and Self-esteem

When we hear individuals talk about affection, how regularly do we consider our essential relationship, the one with ourselves — the one at the core of everything else? Take a brief reprieve to consider how you feel about yourself. Do you love yourself? Furthermore, what does that even mean? Tragically, for a significant number of us, our default mode is self-basic, running just beneath the outside of our activities and communications on the planet. Exploration shows that 50 percent of us aren't self-empathetic; truth be told; we are routinely hard on ourselves. Let's see what causes us to feel that way:

Negative Criticism

Individuals with low self-esteem are too brutal on themselves, and regularly direct emotions towards themselves that they could never say about another person. Negative criticism about one's appearance, knowledge, achievements, and even character just exacerbates the confidence. This gets routine and part of one's convictions about self.

Lack of Family Attention

When we are youthful, our emotions about ourselves are vigorously affected by how others feel about and treat us. Everybody merits a caring family; however, some youngsters have the incident of not getting sufficient help at home. Guardians/parents with psychological well-being issues, substance misuse issues, or different difficulties will be unable to furnish their youngsters with consideration, direction, and thought that they require and merit. This can cause noteworthy confidence issues for youngsters, as those who should think about the most may not appear.

Negative Peers

Similarly, how our family treats us can extraordinarily impact our confidence, so is the effect of peers' treatment on us. Being part of a social gathering that cuts you down – by not regarding you, by constraining you to do things you are not happy with, not esteeming your considerations and emotions, can make you feel like something is not right with you. The main route for you to be preferred is to do what others need, and not easily give in to your own heart and psyche. This is extremely harmful to how you see yourself.

Childhood Abuse

It does not matter whether it is physical, emotional abuse, or a blend of these; it causes emotions of disgrace. While growing up, that child might develop a confused personality. He becomes vulnerable and probably quiet. Childhood trauma and abuse may sometimes leave feelings of numbness. Those people do not know how to handle their emotions. So they distance themselves from others and go into the shell. This leads to having low self-esteem.

Self-perception

Self-perception is a massive factor in youngsters' confidence. For example, when they are perceived, they are encircled by unreasonable pictures of what women ought to resemble, what the perfect body type is. Women's bodies are continually generalized in the media, causing it to appear as their bodies exist for others to see, contact, and use. At the point when adolescence comes around, and our bodies begin to transform, they do not change into what we see in music recordings or magazine covers. This can lead to having serious self-esteem issues. The pressure of having the perfect outlook leads to low-self-esteem. It is the start of rejecting yourself. It does not matter whether we talk about men or women; they equally get affected by the bogus beauty standards. We become what we think of ourselves. When we ill-perceive ourselves, it is more likely that we go into the abyss of negativity and low-confidence.

Lack of Meaning and Purpose

It is simple for people to feel gobbled up in a world outside their ability to control. This prompts emotions of incapability, feebleness, and uselessness. They ask themselves the most difficult questions like: What am I doing here? What difference did I make? A failure to respond to these inquiries can represent a critical test for one's feeling of self-esteem.

Setting Unrealistic Goals

Living in an unrealistic world and setting unrealistic goals in your life may lead to huge disappointment. Youngsters who long for prevalence may anticipate that everybody should like them — something that just does not occur. Regardless of what your identity is, it is not possible to satisfy everybody. The inescapable inability to meet ridiculous objectives may prompt the inclination that you are a disappointment as a rule.

Regret over Past Choices

Maybe you have not been an excellent companion before. Perhaps you did not put forth a concentrated effort in school. Maybe you took an interest in hazardous practices like medication use. You may believe you are only the individual who acts in those ways. You may even feel an abhorrence of yourself necessarily in the view of past decisions. You hold that regret of making some bad choices in your life, and you do not let it go.

5 COMMON WAYS WE KEEP OUR SELF-ESTEEM LOW

Before we dive deep into developing healthy self-esteem and generally what makes a strong character, I want to briefly point out a few common (and usually subtle) ways we lower our self-esteem and make it unhealthy.

Below are five toxic mentalities and behaviors.

These behaviors and mentalities will gradually modify your beliefs about yourself. To the worst!

If you care about your self-esteem, deal with the below list seriously.

Be Hopeless

To believe that your life sucks is already a bad thing. It feels bad. But to believe that your life sucks and you can't do anything about it, that's another level!

It doesn't only feel bad; it feels horrible. This horrible feeling is enough to destroy whatever self-esteem that you have. Let alone that the quality of your life will suffer. Helplessness is about believing that there is no hope. That whatever you do, it won't make a difference. Or worse, that you can't even do anything about your situation. This is the worst belief you can ever adopt in your life. It will destroy you. It's like being convinced that you will be hit by the train because you are laying on the trail with broken legs.

However, there is enough time to crawl out of the trail. There is enough energy in you to hold a rock on the road and pull yourself toward it and out of the trail. There is enough time to call for help from those around you. This might be painful, but it's possible and might save you. But you will surely never do any of that if you believe that you are helpless and that hope has gone. You'll just wait for your destiny and die, thinking that nothing can be done.

Don't ever think this way. It might feel as though. It might be painful to do anything. But you are never helpless, and you can always do something. As long as you are responsible for your life, you always have the choice to step up and do something.

Indulge in Shame

The root of any self-image or self-esteem issue is a shame. Shame says I'm bad. When you feel ashamed, you deeply believe that you are bad. Let's break down what "bad" means. It means that one is unworthy of love, respect, success, or anything that is worthwhile in this world. This means that the person feels that he/she is too bad to be accepted, loved, or appreciated. Shame is about believing that because I have XYZ, I'm not worthy, and I'm bad, and I'll be unloved and rejected. So, I'll hide those XYZ and appear as a perfect individual.

However, perfect individuals don't exist. Those XYZ can be normal human flaws. Or they can be certain bad behaviors or mistakes. Or they can be simply about appearing weak or vulnerable (e.g., if I sucked, it means something is wrong with me). Of course, shame is unproductive and very toxic. Nothing good comes out of it. You must be aware that you are not alone. All of the people you see around you are not perfect. Many people suffer from their problems. They just don't talk that much about them. In fact, most people suffer from similar issues and problems.

So, don't ever feel ashamed because you have a specific issue. For instance, don't feel like you are less than other people because you have some unresolved emotional problems. Every one of us went through specific life situations. Everyone is different. But when it comes to the problems and the flaws and the issues, we all develop them, and we all have our share of them. Work on solving them, but never feel ashamed of them. Never feel ashamed of your shortcomings and imperfections. Feel guilty if you want, but never ashamed. We all have them. And honestly, they don't make you less of a person or less worthy of anything. They only make you a human.

Be a Lazy Couch Potato

I have many stories about laziness. More than I would like to admit. It might not be an issue for some people. At least not as big as shame or helplessness. That is only partly correct. Laziness can, and will, lead to other serious problems and issues. Serious issues related to your self-worth and your life quality.

For instance, writing is my bread and butter. But laziness was, and still, one of the problems that I face as a writer. Though it is hard to admit it, procrastination is something that I have to deal with daily. Maybe one day I'll kick it out of my life. For now, just one day at a time. Because of this seemingly small laziness problem, I've suffered a lot. I feel bad about myself because of the many things I should have done.

Wasting time and procrastination will hurt your self-esteem. It's a bold statement, but it's true. When you looked away from your problems and did not bother fixing them, they will grow bigger. When they grow bigger, bad emotions will kick in. If you don't respond to those bad emotions by taking action, you'll feel bad about yourself. Continuously feeling bad about yourself conveys to your mind the idea that you are not a reliable person, and you'll always suffer because you can't solve your problems.

Laziness is one of the ways we escape our problems and choose not to face them. Too much work threatens us to the point of deciding to do nothing. Break this cycle and decide that you are going to do whatever it takes to get the critical tasks done. You'll thank yourself later. And yourself will thank you by giving you a self-esteem boost. Note that laziness sometimes can be caused by other reasons. Other reasons such as Fear...

Listen to Fear

I hurt my writing by being lazy. I could've written more letters and touched more lives. But it's not only about laziness. In fact, sometimes laziness was induced by nothing but fear. Sometimes I was just lazy. Other times I wasn't lazy; I was scared. I was scared of being judged. I was scared of failure. I was scared of putting something out there that isn't perfect or good enough. Heck, I was even scared of constructive criticism. And I still suffer and haunted from most of these fears every now and then. My first blog failed, and I had to give up on it. And it took me a lot of time to pick myself up again and start publishing articles and show them to people.

Why? Because of fear.

Every day, I overthink my plans but never take any practical steps. I overthink most of the paragraphs I write, wondering if they are good enough. And even after I write them, I don't dare to show them to people. Heck, I've never even realized that until I've written it above!

That fear kept me paralyzed. That fear made me feel weak and made me feel like I'm not the kind of person I want to be. And what's more, that fear made me stuck where I'm and far away from reaching my goals. Feeling like a coward who can't solve his problems sucks. Feeling like you are crippled by fear will make you feel like that coward.

Giving up to fear can screw up your self-esteem as well as your life. Step up and don't listen to that fear. Feel it and go do it as if it's the last thing you're going to do. Forget about doing it perfectly. Forget about the results even. I prefer dying as a warrior in a fight rather than a coward who gives in not to get hurt but get killed anyway.

Hang Around Insecure and toxics People

The people you spend time with will affect you sooner or later. If they are confident and secure, your self-image will become healthier. If they are insecure, you will end up feeling bad about yourself. Generally speaking, do not spend too much time with those who make you feel bad about yourself. Contrary to common belief, insecure people can come in all sizes and shapes. They are not necessarily miserable and weak. They actually can be successful and very charming.

But they drag you down. They make you feel bad about yourself. They manipulate you and emotionally blackmail you. After knowing them for some time, you start feeling that something is wrong. However, you usually still can't get yourself out of the relationship. Whether it is friendship or a romantic relationship, break the cycle. Get those people out of your life. Walk out of their lives.

Most of them are narcissists, emotionally unstable people, or people with bad intentions. Walk away. Don't ever stick around trying to change them or guide them. Walk away if you care about your self-esteem and your mental stability. I've written an article that shows how to know if the other person is the one who is making you feel insecure, or you are already feeling insecure right here.

GIVE LOVE TO YOURSELF

We know and understand the most important relationship in the world is the relationship you have with yourself. The harder you work on this one relationship, the more rewarding life will become, and the better your relationships with other people around you will be.

In order to be more loving towards yourself, I'll suggest that you incorporate rituals into your daily life. The right kind of self-care rituals will help you deepen your relationship with your body, mind, and soul.

One of the most powerful methods and effective ways of connecting with your body is by doing a daily self-massage. In Ayurveda, the ancient process of healing from India, this is known as 'abhyanga.' What's interesting is that the Sanskrit word for oil is 'Sneha.' 'Sneha' also means affection. Hence, the act of performing abhyanga or body massage (with oil) is an act of giving love to oneself.

There is something tremendously healing in the power of touch. When you touch yourself with love and care, you deliver a positive message to your mind – one that reinforces the fact that you and your needs are important. If you do a daily self-massage, then you also become very sensitive to the needs of your body and all the changes that are happening in it constantly. For instance, you will be able to identify the smallest of changes that start taking place in your body before your menstrual period begins to set in. You also learn how to take better care of yourself based on all the signs that your body is providing you.

Doing a self-massage is one of the daily prescriptions given in Ayurveda for maintaining optimal health. It not only relaxes and rejuvenates the body but also puts the mind at ease.

Another practice that I would highly recommend is journaling. There's nothing more effective and powerful than writing down your thoughts, emotions, feelings, and observations on a day-to-day basis. Jim Rohn famously said, "A life worth living is a worth life recording."

No matter what you are going through – how good or challenging your day has been – writing things down will help you put things into perspective. You will be able to develop a deeper understanding of the circumstances that you are currently being presented with. This understanding will help you in coming up with solutions. Looking back at old diary records will also help you remember all the wonderful times you have enjoyed.

I would also suggest that you write down three things that you are grateful for at the end of every day. Sometimes you might think you have nothing to be grateful for, but that's just not true. You could be grateful for the fact that you have a bed to sleep on, a diary to write in, a pen to write with. Some so many people don't even have these basic things and would consider themselves enormously privileged to have your life despite all its challenges.

Gratitude is also the most powerful form of prayer. By saying thank you are making room for the Universe to send you more things to be grateful for. Blessings attract more blessings in life. If you focus your energy on complaining, then you will manifest more of what you dislike.

Be grateful for every experience as it is here to help you learn an important lesson. In fact, if you want to transform the situations of your life, then you must first be grateful and appreciate every experience that you have been presented with. Even if you can't see the silver lining it, trust that it exists. The more negative energy you project onto something, the greater the problem becomes. Thinking of something as a problem is, in itself, an act of magnifying the negativity contained in it.

You must change your mindset because unless you increase your vibrational frequency with gratitude and love, you will keep on attracting challenging situations in life. The people and outer circumstances might change, but the root of the issue will remain the same because every challenge has come in your life to teach you something. The only way you can release it completely is by fully embracing the seed of wisdom that is present in it.

Tasks for This Week:

➤ Start doing a daily full-body massage. Ayurveda recommends using medicated cold-pressed sesame oil for this. I would suggest the time to do this massage is in the morning. It would be ideal if you could make this a daily routine but even if you aren't able to do that, at least aim to do one or two full-body massages every week.

➤ Start and end your day with gratitude. Before getting out of bed, say a small prayer of gratitude in your mind or out aloud. Count at least 3 or 5 things you are grateful for. Every time you encounter a challenge in your day, remind yourself that you must be grateful for the lesson that is brought to you through it. Fully embrace the lesson – allow your heart to pulsate with unconditional love and gratitude towards it. This way, you can transform any circumstance of life.

➤ Get in the habit of daily journaling. At night, write down at least three things you are grateful for. Some days it might be hard to do this practice, but remember that those are the days you need to do this practice even more. When you develop the habit of finding the pearls of wisdom hidden inside every situation of life, you build the ability to face any circumstance of life with tenacity and strength. Also, don't forget that the only way you can attract more blessings in your life is by being grateful for the blessings that you already have in your life.

Love is the most powerful healer. Gratitude is the most powerful magnet that will attract more good things into your life. By performing the physical act of writing down what you are grateful for, you are hardwiring the brain to see the best in every situation. Hence, I encourage you to not just mentally or verbally speak what you are grateful for but also foster the habit of writing things down. This way you are truly internalizing these positive habits. Every day reflect on your day to find the silver lining in everything.

DEALING WITH BAD RELATIONSHIPS

Most people know if they're in a poor relationship, right?

Wrong.

There are thousands of people in bad relationships who don't even realize they're in a bad relationship. You've probably seen it for yourself with friends who refuse to break up with their toxic boyfriend or girlfriend. You don't understand how they could stay in a bad relationship. Take a step back and realize for a second that it could easily be you in their situation. Most relationships are not healthy relationships. Most have huge problems.

There are three kinds of relationships. Codependent relationships, independent relationships, and interdependent relationships. If you keep finding yourself in bad relationships, it's most likely because you're in the codependent section. Codependency is where two people in a relationship use the other as emotional crutches in a relationship. The next level is an independent relationship. Both members are strong on their own, but they don't synergize very well. The last level is the interdependent relationship. The two of them work together and create a sum greater than the whole of its parts.

Most people don't like to admit that they're in a codependent relationship. It sounds like you're enabling the other person. What it really means is that you struggle to be happy and fulfilled on your own.

The reason this happens is that both people in a relationship have flaws that they're not willing to admit to. The problem is found within each of us, not outside of us. This is why it's so tricky because the brain likes to create scenarios where it's the other person's fault. This doesn't mean the other person isn't doing anything wrong, but it does mean that you need to take 100% responsibility for your actions.

You also have to bite the bullet and realize that all your relationship problems won't end the moment you decide to end the relationship. If you have a vision of leaving a bad relationship, finding the right person, and living a happy life together, it will never happen. Unless you're willing to go inside yourself and do the introspective work, it's impossible to have a stable relationship.

Going inside is not easy. It's one of the hardest things you can do. If you want to have a positive relationship, however, you can't overlook introspection.

You need to look inside and see why you need Love so badly. Why don't you feel good enough for yourself? Were you neglected as a youth and denied Love from your guardians? Have you had bad relationships in the past, which ruined your ability to have a positive one today?

Why Self-Love? To Love others, you must be able to Love yourself first. Once you're able to love yourself, you can Love those around you. If you're in a bad relationship, you're not expressing Self-Love as you do not love yourself enough to leave a negative relationship. Self-Love is the most important thing when it comes to having a positive relationship.

HEALING YOURSELF FROM PAST RELATIONSHIPS

When you have spent your whole life caring for other people, looking after their needs, and pretty much-loving everyone but yourself, getting back to self-love is not always easy. Changing from an externally focused person to caring for your own needs is an essential part of your healing process.

The best way to focus inward is to spend some time alone. This will allow you to focus on meeting your own needs without worrying about other people. Whether this means taking a holiday or putting some distance between you and your daily life, do whatever it takes to get some time to reconnect with yourself.

If you have embarked on a new relationship, allow yourself to be loved. It may be strange having someone meet your needs for the first time, but you need to get used to what it means to be in a healthy and balanced relationship. Avoid falling back into old codependent patterns. Always be self-aware and look out for warning signs that you may be falling back to old patterns of behavior.

In your recovery process, do not forget to have fun. Making happy memories can help you get past your old hurts. New happy memories can replace the old sad ones and help you to emerge stronger and more secure in yourself. This is the perfect time to stop whatever you are doing right now and take a look at yourself and rediscover your interests and develop new passions that will let you to get to know yourself much better and have fun as you do it.

When you rediscover what your goals, interests, and passions are. You can plan activities around these three areas that will help you in becoming the best possible version of yourself. Keep in mind that your goal at this point is not just to ditch the old codependency tendencies, but to create new healthy habits that will keep you occupied on the road to bettering your life.

One of the issues and obstacles you may face is learning to trust and love again. Once we have been through a damaging relationship, it is natural to want to protect ourselves by avoiding intimacy and relationships. Never deny yourself a chance at happiness because you are afraid that history may repeat itself.

Spend time alone as you need to feel whole again but do not give up on love and relationships. Ultimately, relationships make our lives much richer. Sharing your experiences with someone who loves and cares for you is a natural part of a healthy life. Always be open to the possibility of love and trust that you have moved on from codependency.

Overcoming the Fear of Intimacy

We have already tackled some of the fears that may predispose you to become codependent. These are fears like the fear of abandonment, the fear of rejection, and other insecurities. These unresolved issues make it difficult to open up to others and form deep connections with them.

If you are still suffering from codependency or in the process of recovering from codependency, these fears may still plague you. This tells you that you need to find a way to overcome them if you are to have truly open and meaningful connections with people. As long as you remain emotionally unavailable, your relationships will continue to be dysfunctional.

Emotional intimacy goes beyond the physical aspects of your relationships. It is possible to have a physical relationship with someone without being emotionally intimate with them. Emotional intimacy requires complete openness on an emotional level and the willingness to bare your innermost feelings to the other person.

This kind of intimacy breeds a sense of security and safety in knowing that you can be completely true to yourself without needing to suppress or camouflage your emotions. Getting to this point in a relationship is never easy, and it can be especially hard for codependents who have a history of dysfunction and abuse in their relationships.

So how do you get over your fear of intimacy? Is it possible to get past unresolved abandonment issues and trust people enough to let them into your life?

The following are some effective tactics or strategies that will help you get past your fear of intimacy.

1. Identify your triggers

In most cases, your fear of intimacy will be due to unresolved issues from your past. Self-analyzing and identifying what triggers your fear of intimacy will help you address it objectively. Were you neglected as a child? Have a bad relationship that made it difficult to trust other people?

Whatever your trigger is, it is very crucial to realize that unresolved issues only leave you with emotional baggage that affects the health of your potential relationships. Whether it will take some therapy, self-forgiveness or forgiving others to get past your fears, do not ignore your unresolved issues.

Knowing your triggers is the very first step to releasing them. As difficult as it is, facing your unresolved issues is one of the best ways to unburden yourself. Take the first step to dumping your emotional baggage by seeking help for your unresolved issues.

2. Be your own best friend

This is as opposed to constantly criticizing and finding fault in yourself and your actions. The fear of intimacy can be enhanced by low self-esteem that makes you feel unworthy of love. This negative self-image makes you avoid getting emotionally involved to minimize the chance of rejection.

Stop criticizing yourself constantly. Focus on your strengths, and accept your flaws. No one is perfect, and always talking yourself down does nothing but dent your confidence. Every day stand in front of the mirror, then look and find something you like about yourself.

Never allow negative thoughts to dominate your mind. You have the power to construct a positive self-image, but this will only happen if you learn to be kind to yourself. The more self-confident you feel about yourself, the less the fear of rejection that you will experience. This will definitely help you and make it easier for you to open up and take a chance on intimacy.

3.   Find a way to de-stress

Stress tends to amplify our anxiety and minimize our self-confidence. Finding an effective way to manage negative emotions such as stress will help you develop a positive outlook.

Yoga, meditation, and exercise are simple ways to not only boost your confidence but also minimize the stress levels in your life. The happier and comfortable you are, the more open you will be to intimacy.

Taking care of your body also helps to boost your confidence and self-esteem levels which again makes a big improvement in how you view intimacy.

4.   Do you know what you want?

Sometimes our fear of intimacy has more to do with the person we are in a relationship with than with our unresolved issues. If you are not sure the person is right for you, then do not rush into intimacy. Intimacy makes any connection deeper and more meaningful, but it will only work if you are with the right person.

Figure out what you want from a relationship. This will give you the confidence to either become intimate or hold off on it until you are sure of your motives and goals. Indecision can be just as damaging as making the wrong choice so always make a point to identify what you want from a relationship early on.

5.   Practice being vulnerable

Just as you cannot fish from the shore, you cannot overcome your fear of intimacy by avoiding relationships. Put yourself out there and take a chance that you can handle any outcome in your relationship. Start small by initiating contact with someone you like, even if it is just as a friend. The more often you do these acts, the better you will get at letting yourself be vulnerable.

Suppose you are not ready for an intimate relationship. Take small baby steps that will slowly help you get past your fear of intimacy. Start by talking and opening up to close friends and family and get used to being vulnerable and exposed. This way when it is time for an intimate relationship, it will not be as daunting or scary.

Disrupting Self-Defeating Values

Self-defeating behavior is common not just in codependents but in other personality types as well. Self-defeating beliefs or values are a set of traits that reflect pervasive and inflexible traits that we have developed over time. Most of these self-defeating values are developed as self-defense or coping mechanisms to help us deal with our environment and various situations.

Self-defeating values impact your self-confidence and hinder your ability to have healthy relationships. They put you in a continuous cycle of repeating patterns that become the order of the day in your life. Then, you begin to realize that little by little, your life is unfolding in predictable patterns.

The danger of self-defeating values is that the box you into a little corner and minimize your options and opportunities. For instance, if one of your self-defeating beliefs is love addiction, then you will always operate based on a belief that your life only means something when you are in a relationship. This means you will be incapable of conceiving of happiness outside of a relationship.

Self-defeating values are akin to putting a straight jacket on yourself that limits your range of thoughts, emotions, and beliefs.

The following are some common self-defeating values that may be impacting your life.

1. Perfectionism. This may seem like a noble idea, but since perfection is not possible, it only makes you feel bad about yourself. When you are constantly falling short of your unrealistic expectations, your self-esteem is shattered.

2. Achievement addiction is similar to perfectionism. If you have this belief, you have attached your sense of self-worth to achieving certain milestones such as career, income, looks, and so on. Again, this limits your ability to appreciate small victories in your life and sets you up for constant disappointment.

3. Approval addiction is another self-defeating value that predisposes you to codependency. If you have this belief, you get your validation from pleasing and getting acceptance from other people. This is likely to make you over function in other people's lives, which is a classic symptom of codependent tendencies.

4. Blaming. This self-defeating belief breeds the inability to accept responsibility for your own mistakes. In this case, you hold other people accountable for your happiness, your actions, and your mistakes. If you have this belief, you may be manipulative and prone to narcissistic behavior.

5. Self-guilt. This is the opposite of blaming and is a common self-defeating belief in codependents. It allows them to take on other people's problems and take on roles like the enabler and the caretaker.

The problem with self-defeating beliefs is that they can impede our growth by narrowing down our thinking. Our thoughts ultimately become our reality, and your world will only stretch as far as your mind allows it to. If self-defeating values bog down your life, you will find that your life is restricted to a few self-repeating patterns.

Unless you change your beliefs, it will be almost impossible to escape the destructive patterns in your life. You therefore, first need to identify the limitations you have placed in your life with self-defeating beliefs and then actively start to change those beliefs.

The danger of self-limiting beliefs is that they lead to generalizations. This is where you paint all situations in your life with a broad brush and then respond with the pre-programmed response you have trained yourself to use.

EMBRACE YOUR AUTHENTIC SELF

Who are you? What are you like deep down? Do you even know? These are all hard questions to answer if you have been living life on someone else's terms. There is no limit of advice as to how to live your life, but none of that matters if it doesn't fit you. Knowing who you are and what you want are oftentimes much more complicated than knowing what you don't want. So start from there.

Living an authentic life requires scraping away all the limitations you have allowed yourself to believe – like the one that whispers in your ear, "You're not good enough".

Unfortunately, it also requires risk and the very real possibility that people won't like you without the mask. This, in turn, requires the courage to be vulnerable, to fail, to make mistakes, and to be seen – warts and all.

Being courageous is not the same as being fearless. Courage is feeling the fear and the anxiety and going ahead and doing it anyway. Courage is an interesting word because the root is the Latin 'cor', meaning heart. So courage is not bravery as such, but living from the heart by doing what you know in your heart is right. When you live courageously by following your heart, you conquer fear, and that gives you more confidence in your abilities to overcome life's challenges. The word confidence comes from the Latin 'com' (with) and 'fidere' (to trust or have faith in).

So living your truth leads to having more faith in yourself, which in turn leads to more courage and more confidence. It all starts with BEING authentically you, which allows you to DO what your heart calls you to do, and then you HAVE the life you desire because you start to manifest the given opportunities that are in alignment with your heart.

If confidence means with full trust, you have to recognize that trust is never a given. Trust has to be earned! And you earn your own trust by consistently behaving in accordance with your own values – in other words, by being authentically you. The flip side to that is living a lie, which gets you distrust, doubt, and uncertainty. Everyone is original, and you don't need the approval of anyone else but yourself.

As scary as authenticity is, the flip side is much scarier. Trying to be something or someone that you are not, is incredibly draining. Trying to live up to the expectations of others whilst ignoring your own aspirations is tough. Trying to maintain the wrong sense of self and false identity is exhausting because it takes an awful lot of energy. When you attempt to be someone different from who you really are, there will naturally be loads of internal conflict. How can it be any other way? You can't be you, and you can only fake it. As there is only one you, you have no choice but to honor that you accept it and embrace it.

So here's the problem – we live in a society that endorses and encourages non-authenticity. Social media is fabulous, but it also allows people to present all the highlights of their lives and skip over the low points. You can be as picky as you like without being dishonest, except by omission. Advertising and the general media add to this by constantly fostering idealized images of beauty, acceptability, and success, which makes us compare ourselves to others.

When you compare yourself to someone else and feel that you come up short, you deny your uniqueness and the things that make you special. You are rejecting your individuality, and then you start to fit in and to pretend. As most of the world is pretending, putting on, shaming, and presenting their unauthentic selves to the world, you are comparing your life to ones that simply don't exist! Even if someone is being

authentic, you have no idea what challenges that person has faced getting there, what it cost them, and how much work it took.

So just stop the comparisons and put your energy into finding your own voice. The source of all our pain, suffering, and discomfort is the notion that we are not good enough, and we only feel that way by comparison. So really, you have no choice but to be you, the real you. Nobody does you as you do.

Being authentic is admittedly intimidating. On top of that, it's not a once-off; you have to commit to it over and over again. It's something you have to do and keep doing by constantly checking in with yourself and asking, "Do I want to say/be/do this?" This takes awareness.

When I first started podcasting and putting myself out there, I realized I was creating an opportunity to live in my authentic self. This is what people wanted. And to be honest, it was scary. Why? Well, I went from a school system to a working system that required me to act and be a certain way, which usually didn't speak to who I really was.

There are no 'should' to living an authentic life because only you know how that looks for you. You construct and design your life from the inside out by your thoughts, beliefs, and dreams, but you are not your thoughts, beliefs, and dreams because these things can change. The thinker, believer, and dreamer do not change, however. You are always allowed to change your thoughts; in fact, it's mandatory. You can think of different thoughts today from the ones you thought yesterday and contradict yourself and then do it again tomorrow.

If you follow the crowd and conform, you are not allowed to change your mind – your mind is changed for you, and then you have to stay there. Trust yourself to entertain a different perspective and to change that perspective when necessary to let in new ideas and new creations.

Imposter Syndrome

A lot of very capable and effective people are convinced that they are faking it, even when they are successful. These individuals live in constant fear of being exposed as frauds. You would be absolutely amazed at how many people feel like frauds, especially women, and even more so, women of color. From college students to mothers, professionals, CEOs and successful actors and authors, men and women all over the world think that one day someone will find out they are not really talented, they are not completely aware of what they are doing, they shouldn't be doing their jobs, and they don't really belong there.

And it gets worse – the higher up you go and the more successful you become, the more you can feel like an imposter because you realize there is still so much more for you to learn and the goalposts are always moving. This extends beyond the workplace, though. Some people feel like they are just playing house when they give a dinner party or that they aren't really grown up when "adulting".

The imposter syndrome is widespread, and the truth is that everybody is winging it to some degree so we can all calm down. Nobody is perfect, and nobody knows how to do something they haven't done before, so if your job is in any way challenging, there is always going to be some trial of your abilities. We don't get lessons in how to live life, have a kid, launch a business, or get old. Only experience can teach us these things, but things are constantly changing. This includes yourself.

Everything you do is an act of creation as life is a creative process – the question is, are you creating something you want or something you don't want? The only way to get good at something is to apply yourself, make mistakes, learn from them, and try again. If you think that talent is fixed, that you should just know how to do stuff, you hold yourself back unnecessarily. When you realize that talent has to be nurtured and grown and that there will be an endless learning curve, you allow yourself to grow.

Instead of trying to cure the imposter syndrome, recognize it as a normal and natural feeling and welcome it because it means that you are self-aware. The minute you think you know it all is the minute you start to stagnate. Why try harder or try doing things differently if you believe you have already "arrived"? The tension generated by not knowing if you can do something well or at all is very often just the impetus you need to push yourself a bit harder to overcome the challenges and to stretch yourself beyond your current capabilities.

It might sound counterintuitive, but sometimes you just have to drop your standards, stop being so hard on yourself and let go of trying to be perfect. This means you accept that you are inherently flawed and that it's ok! Then you can relax a bit, step into the real you, and bring forth your unique gifts instead of burying them under a bushel of procrastination. Learn to live with the certainty of uncertainty.

POSITIVE IMAGINATION ANDSELF – CONFIDENCE

With this juncture, you've got some notion of how successful your mind is and also the effects your ideas can have on your connection. Your thoughts are powerful, and philosophers have said that what you presume will be exactly what you become. It is then possible to use your creativity to construct your self-confidence in case you've been suffering from jealousy and insecurity.

Using your creativity might bring forward a scenario that you wanted for, but that doesn't exist yet. Remember the way your imagination went crazy when your partner was getting home fifteen minutes late? Well, now's the opportunity to turn that creativity around for the better and utilize it to make yourself feel confident and positive about you.

As an example, you are with your partner in a public place, and you also find a famous person that your partner admires. You're able to view them becoming excited, a smile breaks out on their face, and they're eagerly going in that way; to receive a picture. In case you've got low self-confidence, you might tell yourself that they're only doing this so they can compare one with all the famous individuals.

You could also believe they enjoy the famous person over you, which explains the reason they would like to acquire the picture.

If you're both positive and self-confident, none of these situations is going to be of any issue. You'll have the ability to conclude that this really is a famous person the partner may only have a beat; the risk that they'd leave you for this individual is quite low.

Then, you'll evaluate your positive features and the way you bring about the connection. From the time you've finished this mind game and avoided the situation that does not have any foundation to fret about, your loved one would have gone and return to show you with enthusiasm the autograph they have received.

For each action, there's an equivalent response, and this is relevant to your own feelings. If you would like to feel great, then you might do things that make you feel great. This straightforward analogy can definitely help you grow your confidence readily.

Jealous activities, anxiety attacks, and bursts of bitterness, these are feelings that don't feel great, and they need to be prevented. Loving ideas, planning for love, trusting your partner, thinking about these emotions make you feel great. Acting on those ideas should bring more sense of superior situations into your own space.

To feel more convinced, you've got to forego the payoff which you get from insecurity. This might seem like a strange or awkward statement, particularly once you understand that jealousy is what we refer to as the most adorable side of your character. Occasionally, whenever you exhibit your insecurity, you receive more love from the spouse, they take the time to allay your fears, and they might even go out of the way by trying to explain to you just how much they genuinely love you.

For example, you're out for dinner, and you see that for a split second, your boyfriend/girlfriend is admiring another individual. Since you pout and move quiet, your partner starts to profess his/her love to assure you that it's you that he/she loves, not another individual.

Then they're on their very best behavior for the remainder of the day, which makes you feel great. They get you flowers after dinner and get you a present on the way to the house in order to apologize. They keep asking if you're okay and take accountability for their split-second glimpse. They feel guilty and thus will do anything to make you grin.

This may be quite addictive, and you might get stuck in a perpetual pity party, where you begin to search for situations that will bring your insecurity out. In case you're more confident and have a much better self-image, then your companion will love you by a stage of admiration as opposed to as a consequence of guilt.

You will still get the love, and it's very likely to be genuine that it was earlier. So, let's try an exercise: Locate a serene, quiet spot to sit, close your eyes, and imagine that you're totally relaxed. Now, imagine a scenario that would cause you to feel envious, really jealous, then deepen your breathing. Make sure your limbs are relaxed, and your heart rate slows as you envision that terrible circumstance. An amazing means to get this done is to imagine that you are disinterested in that specific circumstance.

The circumstance is distinct from you and doesn't state anything about you as an individual. It doesn't indicate you are not as desirable or less appealing. It's just you interpreting what you've seen your husband/wife perform. You are aware that your creativity can run away from you, so you choose to allow the whole situation to go. Send it into the deepest recesses of your mind and totally ignore it. It's not more significant than you, and it definitely doesn't define you.

This can allow you to take away the energy with that circumstance, thus returning the ability to you. The final product is going to be your creativity being under management, and you'll realize that you genuinely have the capability to manage the circumstance properly. This will immediately raise your self-confidence, and it's all in your mind. Bear in mind that you're just, ever in charge of yourself and your activities, and you can't control another human being, even if you attempt to do so.

The more you are ready to do this deep breathing and serene detachment when you find yourself in a situation that causes you to feel anxious or jealous, the better you'll feel in your partnership with your significant other. Where there were feelings of stress, there'll be feelings of confidence. Where you're likely to get angry with your girlfriend/boyfriend, you're more inclined to talk about your emotions confidently, in order to bring about mutually beneficial outcomes.

When you're more confident in your relationships, then you create an upset from the dynamics along with your connection that has no choice except to grow into something fantastic. The expression of jealousy is much more about self-improvement than focusing on the feelings of the others.

It's about how you're feeling at the moment instead of taking into account how others feel, and that's the reason why compassion is so essential. When you're confident in yourself, you are less likely to encounter jealous feelings, and in case they appear, you will quickly have the ability to conquer them.

So, in order to be able to conquer jealousy, you will need to get a healthy dose of self-esteem. Finding out how to overcome jealousy isn't about earning your partner change their behavior, it's about you having the ability to conquer your behavior and find out that you're feeling a particular way for yourself rather than somebody else.

Assembling your self-confidence isn't something that happens within a moment, even though you can take action that can show you instant outcomes. It requires a while, and you should approach it one day at a time, and one thought at a time. To build your confidence and envision yourself along with your sport, you can earn some positive affirmations on a daily basis. Try out the following:

- I'm handsome or beautiful and worthy of love.

- There's something about me that's pretty unique.

- The best thing about being me is that I'm totally unique.

- I have got a lot to offer to the entire world.

- I might have a positive effect on my connection.

- I understand I can do great now.

There's power in talking positivity in your own life and your situation, and you've got the capacity to build yourself so you can assist your relationship. In order to attract more positivity in your connection, you have to act in a more favorable manner. This involves you trying to find the good side from both the relationship and on your partner. The real test to build confidence and overcoming jealousy and stress will come about whenever you're facing a challenge on your connection. It's incredibly effortless to lay blame, to accuse, to yell, and to be appropriate at a specific circumstance. It's a lot more challenging to check out the situation positively, as well as in struggles and bring out the very best of yourself. If you can understand how to do so, then you are able to pull in much more positivity to your connection.

5 Simple Things You Can Do in order to Help Adopt a Positive Attitude

Knowing that you want to adopt a favorable mindset is one thing. Reading about the way it is possible to try out a couple of things to help enhance your self-confidence is just another one. Sure, two of these things can help your connection, but they're not the only things you can do to attract more positive and less negative within your relationship.

Maintaining a positive attitude towards life in general, not only in your relationship, will help significantly in regards to getting on your insecurities. Thus, with that being said, here are just five easy things you can do in order to embrace a positive mindset.

Know What You Need to Change

In order to embrace a positive attitude in life, generally, you want to understand what has to be shifted on your own. Being able to identify what has to be changed is not that simple; it will definitely require some fairly profound soul searching. You need to actually look at your character traits to choose which ones you need to work on and finally shift them.

Adopt a Role Model

One of the simplest methods to embrace the mindset that you wish to have would be to find somebody with the same mindset as you. Today we aren't saying to stem this individual and take over their own life, but see and learn by them. Watch how they respond to certain conditions and take your cues from them in order to help yourself better as an individual.

Consider How This Will Change your Life

To be successful in adopting a new lifestyle change, you want to know exactly how it will change your life. Everything you have to do is sit and consider how taking a positive attitude will impact your existing way of life. Start by asking yourself the obvious questions, for example, if the new mindset will cause you and your partner happier or if it's going to make things more agreeable in your own household commonly. As soon as you've answered those questions, keep reminding yourself of the favorable outcomes of the mindset change in order to make sure your success will be achieved.

Make Sure you Carefully Pick Who You Desire

Your buddies have an immediate effect on your mindset. If you surround yourself with negative people, you will have no prospect at all of adopting a positive mindset. This can actually be easier said than done since it sometimes entails drastic lifestyle modifications. You have to carefully assess the folks you surround yourself with and ask if they'll be useful in your journey to embrace a positive mindset. If they are counterproductive for your target, you'll have to decide on whether to cut them from your life or not. Nevertheless, it would help if you remembered that surrounding yourself with positive-minded folks makes it a lot easier to produce the change on your own.

FOR SELF-LOVE, LET GO OF THE POSITION HOLDING YOU BACK

The most valuable lesson I've discovered about Life Coaching is "Who I am." I realized that change is constant, and I'm continuing my learning curve and evolving as a better person for myself by putting myself in a learning environment. The first thing I learned was to let go of worrying for others to the disadvantage of my well-being.

Girls are brought up to love, defend, and, therefore unintentionally neglect the basic obligation of self-care. It is normal for women to feel that they must first take care of others before themselves. This conviction is so deep and powerful that they don't know how to let go of old beliefs that don't match the lifestyles of the 21st century. It's about letting go of having to be all to everyone's positions.

Letting go of the roles of mum, wife, and daughter becomes particularly challenging when we've been performing such positions for a long time. We become so addicted to those positions when we get tired that we no longer know how to participate in other tasks. It is like sacrificing our "identity" to fulfill certain positions. Every position we play today, question ourselves, "Is this what we stand for?" If we're upset, perhaps it's time to rediscover a new "you!" Both individuals have blind spots, and behaviors, and routines are there. Letting go needs someone to explain what we need to "let go." How can I let go? In particular, what do we need to let go of this "sweet spot" first? After letting go of disempowering behaviors and beliefs, with what can we replace them now?

Sometimes when I try to explain that we first need to value ourselves, certain people immediately grasped it; others are going to say, "Isn't that selfish?" Okay, if you first don't fill your cup and then go on filling in others, the cup can dry up early. There's nothing left to share. Self-love is about your own wellness, nutrition, spiritual, emotional, and well-being. Others will be motivated by how you look for yourself and value yourself as you do it. They'll want to do the same as well. The key to happiness is self-love.

My belief is, "God helps those who improve themselves." In other words, others are motivated by your way of living as you lead an inspirational existence. First of all, respect yourself. The key to happiness is self-love.

How Women should "Self-Love" their path to personal liberation and honest speech People with whom I talk and mentor told me what I believe is the key to satisfaction, and my response is always the same, "self-love." Occasionally I tell chocolate-covered caramel with a touch of sea salt when I'm in a playful mood, but let me remain here on the topic.

It is during these discussions that I can always look into the eyes of a woman and see her focus change simply as she sees me prioritizing self-love above all else. It's like being lost in translation somewhere along the way. From what is being written, "Selfish" is being said... And the sad part is, it makes perfect sense to mislead.

Women are trained from girlhood to be caring and treatment vocal externally. While little boys are allowed to smash their Tonka trucks into the baseboards, the comfort of caring for Dolly is often taught by little girls... Feed her, adjust her, give her makeup.

Choose one of today's world's seven plus billion people who haven't got their start from a woman. Also, women who have never given birth for whatever cause are still heavily involved in caring for and maintaining the position of godmother, auntie, mom, niece, tutor, neighbor...

And this is not to say that men are not caretakers and nurturers who are committed, many are, but they do not tend to lose themselves in the role.

The "them first, never mind me" tape that can bog our headspace is harder for women to turn off. In the number of times a day we hear our name called given a reference to "needs," we have the strength, authority, and knowledge to fulfill; we may even go so far as to find value.

Being based on it feels good. That is until there is no other thing.

So, what about recovery?

Sleep's inevitable consequences are even delayed for those who refuse to sleep, taking mental notes of the infamous "undone" while still pledging dedication to the potential "hots" that will eventually demand attention.

Listen, it's not your invitation to fatigue. Neither is severity. And if tiny bits of anger starts creeping in through the cracks of that battered woman's symbol on your face, then that's not just more evidence you're not a savior, it's confirmation you need a savior. Let your self-love come to your rescue.

From a turnip, you can't get blood.

If you only have $10 and I'm asking you for $10.10, you're not enough. You might set your sights on saving, gambling, or doing a steady two-minute cartwheel to raise the other dime, but you don't have enough right now. The same is valid when you first seek to do all that caring, supporting, and being there for everyone else with little preparation in place to develop and display self-love.

It's not news. Everyone knows that you can't give away something you don't already have. It's called fraud in many circles, but we act as if we got a pardon from somewhere when it comes to women and our need to meet needs. We haven't.

And so, how does it feel like this self-love anyway? Does it have anything to do with holding the chocolate mentioned above personal stashes? What about bubble baths every week? Or the owner of a German car? How about our own "true" red bottom shoes coveting?

The marketing and advertising system wants us to believe it, but I strongly beg to differ.

It's self-love...

Self-love is about equality of the feelings. There is no need for other people to acknowledge what a valuable and amazing addition you are to the universe, but to be confident in your understanding of your importance whether or not "they" toot your horn in celebration.

It's about being able to appreciate and enjoy yourself. It's about discovering yourself curious enough to discover the deep knowledge of who feeds your mind, and then respect yourself enough to let it into your life. Knowing what activities will make you feel awesome and warm, and then allowing yourself to mark as many occasions as you can by doing whatever they are.

Self-love respects and acknowledges the wishes, strengths, and abilities of your spirit. Unapologetically.

It takes time to discover what you want to learn so that you remain genuinely interested and invested in what you have called your life. It is sure that your judgment is noble and important enough to indulge in the interactions and partnerships that can only progress you into the pleasure of smiling your belly's take-your-breath.

Self-love is about understanding where you are at the moment and an unwavering and genuine appreciation for who you are at all times. It strokes the folds of your tummy fat and likes it because it's there without judgment and gently reminds you that you can (and will) let it go when you're done.

Self-love is a strong self-reflection that, like an alert discerning bodyguard, radiates in your universe. Any person, place, or thing that does not serve your highest good must give up its power and right to hold the space when you have it. Quickly.

So, all this (and more) is self-love, but where does it come from?

Lord, God. Yeah, yeah? I say I hope, I mean... That sounds like religious programming nowadays, but please listen to me because I have an addendum resurrecting this response from cliché graveyards into full-blown life.

And it is definitely a redemption that we need because the fact of self-love is honesty from a relationship with God. It is as alive today as it has ever been, so the regeneration is our connection to the world.

The second we make up our minds as women that we are willing to go all in and decide to develop the real deal, self-love, is the very second we have to unleash the tradition of addressing God in ancient religious postures. Praying the same old prayers that we have chanted since we were knee-high to a duck is not going to produce the crop that we are after here.

If the goal is self-love...

If self-love is the target, the pose must be true surrender, true readiness to be guided into the depths of the chaos of who we became and why, in whom we permitted ourselves to be transformed while we concentrated on escaping the wilds of a planet that seemed not to matter.

When the target is self-love, we women wail deep prayers like, "God, teach me how I am" and "show me who I am." We pray that way because we realize that self-consideration and redemption is the only path in and out, and we have been squeezed internally for far too long now out of the too little lives.

And then buckle in for your life's ride as this pursuit of self-love is simply not for the weak. Within 1 Corinthians, the popular chapter of love? Okay, get ready to see each of the stuff that true love doesn't do.

Get ready to see yourself puffed up, a restless, quest for your own, and score for you! This process of emotional maturity thing is wild watching it play out!

That's why you have to remember to remember that forgiveness is the biggest step towards love, even self-love.

To receive the light of God in your dark places is all part of His guidance. Jesus hasn't sent a Savior to us because we didn't need one. He sent us a savior because we were doing something!

So trusting in the process of sanctification and remembering that God loves you anyway, has always been the remedy through it all to beat yourself as you grow in self-understanding, acceptance, and love.

God's true love and forgiveness, and Christ's desire for you as a person, is the only thing in existence that is deep and enduring enough to bridge the gap between self-accusation and guilt that is so quickly besetting and self-love that needs to be developed if you want to offer yourself permission to succeed and become what God created you.

But it's not going to happen!

Self-love is not a quality of being that arrives naturally with the knowledge of the Born Again as much as I wish it did. It is the sacred pearl of the Empire, the one of great value to be purposefully found, collected, and maintained above all else.

It is the Good News that I know the Bible is all about: you are set free and empowered to seek, accept, and grow a greater love for yourself without fear of rejection or defeat because of the sacrifice of Jesus.

And as you develop in that passion, it will expose you to the richness of your own honest identity where you and everyone in your love and power circle will gain in the most beneficial ways.

It's not self-love.

Pursue it and wear it proudly as a favorite garment because you will start to see yourself stronger, more purposeful, and more confident, more creative and bolder, more forgiving, more radiant, and freer!

You are going to grow into your God-made selves more and more: God's magnificent mother created you to be!

SETTING BOUNDARIES AND LEARNING TO SAY NO

I've been struggling with feelings of guilt when I tell someone "no" ever since I can remember. I recall how some of my close friends would stop playing with me if I didn't get them the snacks they wanted, and it made me feel heavy inside because I know that they were upset with me.

It's been so ingrained in me that even until now, I still feel heavy inside whenever I have to tell someone "no," but I also know that I have to put my own needs first and I respect myself enough to know not to give any more than I'm willing to give.

Defining Your Boundaries

Saying no to somebody can sometimes take a lot more effort and can be a lot more complicated, especially when it is someone of authority like your boss when they are asking you to do something that's beyond your job description. However, there are plenty of ways in which you can refuse and set firm boundaries without feeling guilty and without getting the other person upset.

First, you have to learn and understand to respect yourself and understand that you are not responsible for other people's problems, and you are not required to give them anything that you're not willing to give. This is, of course, assuming that the other people we're referring to aren't your kids or anyone you're legally or professionally responsible for.

Next, you have to be firm and unrelenting in your refusal. You have to resist the urge to give in no matter what and not even once because that's how other people learn to acknowledge your limits and respect your boundaries. Always remember that what you allow is what will continue.

Make it clear what you are willing and not willing to do from the beginning and stand by it. That's how you gain respect.

Even if you have set boundaries, there will still be people who will try to test those boundaries. I know that it can get annoying when someone keeps on pestering you with the same request over and over. But, it never gives you an excuse to be rude. There are ways for you to refuse without being rude or offending people and that's what we'll be discussing next.

The Art of Saying No

In most cases, you actually do not have to say the word "no." You just have to say "yes" a little less often. You need to be more aware and be more careful about the things that you agree to.

If you automatically say "yes" to any request that is asked of you, then this applies to you perfectly. Being a yes-person may have allowed you to avoid a lot of conflict in the past, but you probably also got left feeling used or abused.

If the word "no" rarely comes out of your mouth, you can start the process now by not agreeing to any non-important, non-urgent request for the next 24 hours. Just tell anyone asking you a favor that you'll think about it and that you will get back to them tomorrow. This should give you the time to really think things over and see if it's something you want to give or not. It also gives you time to come up with a polite way to refuse, should that be what you decide to do.

Continue the process of giving things time before you agree and change your default answer from "yes" into "hold on" or "I'll think about it" then try not to give the other person a chance to convince you to give an immediate answer by telling them that you'll talk about it again once you've had the chance to think.

If the idea of confrontation is still too difficult as you become too nervous and will still respond with a "yes," try to write out your response. This can be through a written letter, email, or text message. It gives you more control, and you will have the opportunity to say exactly what you want to say without forgetting any details, which may happen when you're under the pressure of a face to face situation.

Remember that when you are telling someone "no," there is no need to be mean and aggressive. You are exercising your personal boundaries, and it is within your rights as a person, but remember that other people have feelings too. It would help if you simply said that it is not going to work out. You can also add that you will get back to them once you're in a better situation to help them out. You will find that keeping it simple usually works out best. Just keep any responses lighthearted and be honest about your reasons. They do not need to hear a long story about your life that makes you unable to grant their request.

If you start feeling guilty, keep in mind that when you tell anyone "no," this is not necessarily a reflection of how you feel about this person or what they really mean to you. It's rarely personal as sometimes things just cannot work with your current situation.

Sometimes, instead of a flat out refusal, you can help the person requesting to find an alternative solution or maybe point them in the direction of someone else who may be able to help them.

Do not beat around the bush and just say what you feel in a polite manner. If you are not interested in doing the favor, say "no." A common mistake, other than saying "yes" to something you do not want to do, is indulging the need to explain your reason for rejecting the request fully.

Of course, it is your choice to tell the person the "why," but it should be kept short and should not be a long dialogue about everything that has gone wrong with your life.

Sometimes you have to make long explanations, but if it's not something that you absolutely have to do, then it's always best to keep your refusals short and polite.

The more you say "no" to requests that you don't agree with, the easier it gets over time. You will start to take back control of your life, giving yourself the time that you need to perform your tasks and save your resources for yourself. You have to remember to take care of yourself first before you start worrying about others. Putting yourself first should eventually place you in a better position to help other people.

It's not always easy to assert your own needs, to speak honestly about what you want or don't want, and to put your needs in front of others. You may think that you are not a good person when you tell someone you care about that you are not able to do something for them. But, you also have to believe that if these people care about you, they should also be able to understand your situation and accept your refusal.

SELF-FORGIVENESS

Self-forgiveness is a process in itself, not a technique for working on issues. Often, saying, "I forgive myself" is the modest and straightforward act that allows you to harvest years of good work. Self-forgiveness teaches the basic self how to change, and invites the higher self to foster change. Self-forgiveness is experienced, experienced, but not easily explained. The mind cannot understand. The basic self is stuck in duality and guilt. Self-forgiveness engages the heart and the higher self. It is an active Love that will dismantle self-judgments, mistaken beliefs so that Love takes its place.

Forgive yourself for failing. When we ask for forgiveness, it is because we have cheated on someone else, or we have made a mistake so great that others are affected by it. But why ask forgiveness without forgiving yourself beforehand? Many times we leave many of the responsibilities that we should bear in the hands of others. Here, for example, forgiving. A much clearer example: to love. Is it not true that if we do not love ourselves, we cannot love others? So it's the same with forgiving. Perhaps you are wondering why none has ever taught you this before, why none has ever told you that you must forgive yourself, and then forgive others. The truth is that we have always learned to be "irresponsible" in a way, for our actions. This is one of the reasons why we permit ourselves to love others without first loving ourselves. We want them to forgive us without us having forgiven ourselves before, we demand respect before respecting ourselves, etc.

Fear of forgiving yourself. Perhaps this error into which we fall, the one that prevents us from forgiving ourselves, is only proof of our great fears: to be at alert for our weaknesses and knowing that we are not perfect. It takes a lot to look within and accept our mistakes. Maybe that's why we prefer to look elsewhere. I would like to give some advice so that you can pardon yourself without fear and that when next you have to ask for forgiveness, you will think of yourself first.

Because it is not selfish, in this case, to think of yourself first. You are the most important, and therefore you must begin by asking your forgiveness. Why you have to forgive yourself? You have to know if you have to forgive yourself because sometimes we feel guilty when we are not. Once you are certain of your guilt, you must forgive yourself. But how? Failure doesn't turn you to a bad person: we all make mistakes, and that does not make us horrible beings. So we have to admit our flaws, learn from them, and forgive ourselves. We are human beings, and we are wrong. It's normal! Try again: sometimes we are afraid to start again, but maybe this is the initial step after forgiveness. Think that forgiving yourself is learning; it is rectifying; it realizes where we were wrong. From there, you can begin a new life. Forget the past: maybe you are tormented by these mistakes that you made and that they are still present today. Don't torture yourself with it. Forgive yourself! Use all of these stones in your way to being a better person. Be responsible for your actions: asking for forgiveness is sometimes an irresponsible act because we want to free ourselves from a burden too easily. But if you pardon or forgive yourself before, it's not that simple anymore. Be responsible for your mistakes because you are the person who made them!

Steps to forgive yourself. Sometimes it is more complicated and hard than forgiving someone else. When you live with a feeling of guilt for something that should happen in the yesterday, this bunch of negativity buried deep within you can cause an eternal and penetrating sense of grief. Forgiving yourself is a principal act to move forward and free yourself from the antiquity.

You must understand the importance of forgiveness. Being in a scenario where you are unable to forgive brings the number of energy. The fear of your vulnerability continually crushes you, you burn with anger towards the source of your suffering, and you continuously live in a depressing states such as sadness, pain, and guilt. This energy deserves to be better used so that your creativity, your abilities, and your skills are nourished instead of your negativity. Forgiveness also permits you to exist in the present instead of living in the past, allowing you to move on into the future with a new sense of purpose that will keep you focused on change, improvement and use benign from past experiences, rather than being held back by past wounds. Some are afraid of forgiving themselves because they are scared of missing the meaning of their existence as a self, which has been developed on anger, resentment, and vulnerability. In this case, ask yourself if you need to show yourself to the world as an angry, easy to hurt, and very responsive person. It is enough to go for a limited period of insecurity while you find your way back than to continue living the remainder of your life crushed by anger. See forgiveness positively. If you are embarrassed by the idea that forgiveness means that you should no longer feel intense feelings like resentment and anger, tell yourself that forgiveness can be a chance to experience intense positive emotions like joy, generosity, and self-confidence. Thinking about what you will gain, preferably than what you will lose, has the advantage of keeping you positive while minimizing negative emotions.

Consider the challenges of not forgiving yourself.

The inability to forgive finds its source in anger and resentment, two feelings that can destroy your health. Plenty of researches have proven that people who are stuck in constant anger are extra prone to be sick than people who can learn to forgive themselves and others. Never forget that merciful does not determine overlooking. You have the right to learn from and be guided by your experiences. The goal is to put aside the self- imposed resentment and rebuke that comes with remembering the past. Accept your feelings. Not being able to accept you are feeling like anger, vulnerability, fear, and resentment are part of your struggle. Instead of trying to avoiding these feelings, facing these bad feelings, accept them as part of what strengthens your lack of forgiveness for yourself. A named problem is a problem ready to be solved. Think about why you are attempting to keep yourself higher than anyone around you. Perfectionism can push you to have criteria that are too harsh to judge your behavior, principles that you will not force onto anyone else. If perfectionism makes you be too hard on yourself, you are stuck in a situation where self- forgiveness becomes very hard to give, because it will resemble an acceptance of a lower level self. This enables you to believe that we are all imperfect and that you are human and, therefore, flawed too. If you are struggling with your perfectionism, consider getting counseling or therapy to reduce its influence on your life.

Stop thinking about what others expect or think from you. If you're stuck in a spiral of self-hatred that you never feel up to because of things you've been told, self-forgiveness is important. No one has control over what other people do and say, and a lot of things are said and done subconsciously and often motivated by the faults of others. Spending your time putting yourself down because you consider you are not living up to the expectations of others, is giving too much importance to what another person, with his mixture of feelings, can think. Forgive yourself for trying to meet the expectations of others and, instead, start making the necessary changes to be able to pursue your objective. For every person who has been hard on you, think that an individual has been hard on that person too. Destroy the cycle of severity by being kind to yourself and others and trying not to want to live by the expectations someone else would have of you. When someone randomly criticizes you, realize that this person has just made their life harder if they make a mistake or if they fail to stay at the level of their perfectionist ideals. At that time, remember where you came from and why you no lengthier need to live like this.

Stop punishing yourself. According to a common misunderstanding, forgiveness means forgetting and forgiving. This misunderstanding can cause a person to feel that it is not fair to forgive himself because if he does this, it would be like forgetting and /or showing indulgence towards the past evil if this is what is keeping you back from forgiving yourself, remember that forgiveness is a process of self-awareness in which you continue to remember what happened: you don't suddenly become forgiving and don't start to think of something "bad" as something "good Train" yourself to accept yourself as you are. You don't have to forgive yourself for being yourself. Self-forgiveness is about targeting what makes you feel bad, not about condemning yourself as a person. Self-acceptance as a forgiveness procedure allows you to recognize that you are an accurate person, even with your faults. This does not suggest that you ignore the flaws or that you try to stop changing and improving, but rather that you value more yourself above these elements and that you stop letting your weaknesses slow you down in life.

Love yourself and let others heal you. Laugh more, and it will give you more freedom to prevent using everything so seriously. Think about what will get better in your life if you permit also go how you can make it work. In the process of self-forgiveness, it is usually not enough to just decide to forgive yourself. Doing things to confirm the process of self-forgiveness will help you achieve self-forgiveness and give you a new sense of purpose. Among the things you can think of are:

Start meditation. Meditation is an ideal way to find inner, calm, and spiritual self- realization, in addition to good physical relaxation. This will give you time for yourself and allow you to take in perception with the present moment and enjoy it, but also to become an impact with your inner "you". If you do it consistently, the examination will develop your welfare and knowledge of self. Assert your worth. Usually, retrieve that you are an esteemed and lovely person and just say to yourself, "I pardon myself" or "I won't let anger eat me up again from the inside" as soon as the negative feelings reappear. Have a diary. Describe your journey to remission. Having a space to write, where you can share your thoughts and feelings, which no one else will read, is a liberating and self-revealing way to break down negative approaches to life. Get therapy. If you've really tried to avoid anger, resentment, and other fearful and out of control emotions, but still struggle, contact a therapist who can help you find a better life. If therapy is not right for you, find at least one friend (or more friends) to talk to who can help you assert your worth. If you are a believer, learn from your religion the strength to help you.

WHAT DOES SELF-CONFIDENCE HAVE TO DO WITH FORGIVENESS?

We must remind ourselves who we need to forgive when we lack self-confidence. Forgiveness frees us from the fetters that hold us back. We're freed from the past from our jails.

You are tied to the person or event which harms you through an emotional bond if you hang onto a past hurt. The only way this connection can be broken is by redemption.

Forgiveness is a gift to use for our own higher good. By how much we have been hurt, we no longer define our lives, but by how much we have grown.

It doesn't say we're getting others off the hook scot-free if we forgive. This means we're going to let ourselves off the line. We should go forward with a confidence that is not compromised by what has occurred in our history.

For too long, holding onto a grudge only increases our sense of injustice and keeps us stuck. We see the one that affects us for what they were, although they may have gone on and who knows how to become a much more beautiful person than they were before.

With a new perspective, we will start rebuilding our lives. In reality, we will begin to accept what happened to us and see things from their point of view if we genuinely forgive someone. We have had to struggle inside to do what they've achieved. It can be extremely powerful when we realize this.

That means we can choose to accept any painful experience we face when we go through our lives. We won't hold on to us by sacrificing others in the system, and we won't give up our strength. No one should ever be permitted to take away our strength.

We will restore our faith and self-esteem after we have forgiven others for past hurts. We can choose fresh, stronger values. This will allow you to move from staying to the point of self-power (or inner strength) that allows you to live the life that we were born to live.

There are two aspects to the cycle of reconciliation-to forgive us for what they have done or what we thought they have done to us and to forgive us for feeling negative about them and having them influence us.

Say yes to forgive and get out of the memory. Ultimately, the energy is at the moment. You could make a life of yourself.

How High self-esteem and self-confidence may attract better things into your life

Lack of self-confidence and self-esteem may make it difficult to be effective in many ways. At work, you can find it hard to speak up, you might feel awkward to ask for support, you might feel incapable for raises and pay increases. It can affect the amount of commitment you make when you believe you're not going to get anywhere; you can feel like' why bother.' In marriages, it can contribute to mentally and physically embracing and keeping up with abusive spouses. It can contribute to extreme feelings of insecurity that fan the fires of envy, anger, and a variety of negative words from other relationships. It can even stop you from starting a relationship in fear of getting hurt, or because you're feeling' not good enough.' In social groups, sometimes it can be hard to feel like you fit in with your peers, and it can make it hard to make new friends. It can stop you from doing as much as you want for fear of not being successful, not like how you look and feel about yourself, and just not feel confident in many types of social circumstances.

Within the school environment, a lack of trust can have a direct effect on how well you are doing and also how well you are doing. It can lead to decreased concentration levels and a lack of interest. It can also encourage harassment, of course, because those kinds of people who get an ego boost by throwing others around, mentally or physically, will know you're not going to stand up for yourself.

But be told, you will surely do something about it!

Confidence isn't something you either have or don't have; it's something you can learn and develop when you handle it in the right way. Many people are confident in some areas of their lives, but not in others, and sometimes a confident person might encounter a negative event and have their confidence ' shaken' or' knocked,' which may lead them to be less comfortable in the future in the same situation. All this is perfectly normal. You can also improve and develop your self-esteem, and the two can be easily worked on together.

True self-confidence and self-esteem are not milestones instantly, it may take some time, but how much you want it; it will decide how far you get there.

What are the advantages of increased self-confidence and higher self-esteem?

Picture this way of your living. You are waking up every day, feeling healthy and full of energy, looking forward to the day ahead, understanding that your day is going to be enjoyable for the most part. Don't get me wrong, we all have' ordinary' days, but being able to deal with them and not having them to turn through bad weeks and bad years is a tremendous benefit to reap from increased self-confidence and higher self-esteem.

You are feeling relaxed, secure, and confident with your partner's partnership. Understanding that you are valued for who you are and how you are, without the need for endless public reassurance and the opportunity to provide your companion with the same in exchange. Comfortable speaking about all kinds of things, even the tough subjects which pop up from time to time and are able to express yourself and your thoughts without necessarily having to be right, and causing yourself to be railroaded into anything that you don't want or comply to.

Completely calm and convenient to meet new potential partners and compliment your life. People are often drawn to those who are self-confident (not over-confident, which appears to sit amid arrogance), but sometimes when you lack confidence, you end up joining the' right' form of relationships because the affection you get when you first encounter someone is an internal source of confidence which enhances you, but these partnerships often end up as hard as possible.

Having immense pleasure from having relationships with your friends and family that are more fun. Feeling respected and valued as an adult in your own right, and engaging confidently in all kinds of social events and activities with ease, allows it effortless to build a lively, enjoyable social life.

Being the most you in your life, being more concentrated, prepared and able to deal with challenges as they surface and being able to create a balanced work/life balance can all result in you finding more time to do the things you want to do and have more time with the people that care in your life.

You are getting a fantastic sense of self-worth and achievement from being more productive and efficient at work and being able to interact with people at all levels and from all walks of life comfortably. All of this can lead to greater success in your work life, or better yet, have confidence in your abilities to go out and get the kind of job you'd love to do if you haven't done it already.

Feeling like life never' lets you down' and' stresses you out' because you can deal with challenges, struggles, and losses much more intensely. Understanding that your self-worth is not bound up with outside events, thoughts, or perceptions gives you a great sense of control over your daily life.

Believing in yourself, your ability and judgment allow you to take calculated risks in your personal and professional life, embark on journeys of excitement and anticipation rather than fear and anxiety, and try to achieve everything you want from life, both internally and externally.

It's not about being the party's life and soul, the one with the most to tell, the greatest at all, the highest earner, or the most' things' holder. It's about feeling confident in yourself, safe in the knowledge that you don't need the support or consideration of anyone else to be satisfied.

It's about being totally happy with who you are, what you're doing, and how you're behaving, realizing you're your best self at any given time and recognizing you're a work in progress, as we are all. It's a very convenient way to be.

Evidence has shown that positive self-confidence development and higher self-esteem by coaching can be significantly improved.

Contrary to alternative methods, the powerful way of coaching interacts with you as a person brings in major and lasting improvements in every area of your mental and physical commitment to trust.

Without doing the inside work, the outcomes are rarely going to be permanent.

Assertiveness is the ability to stand up for your rights without being hostile or defensive; the connection between assertiveness and self-confidence. Usually, people who are not assertive let go of their privileges and finally feel poor.

Not only does a lack of assertiveness result in anger buildup, but it also degrades self-confidence. There is a very strong connection between assertiveness and self-confidence to the degree that without being assertive, an individual cannot become truly confident.

I explained before that self-confidence is created as your subconscious mind examines your actions and starts to believe you, therefore assertiveness and self-confidence are closely related.

Of starters, if you've managed to do well enough times in a certain sport, your subconscious mind will start to believe you're good at it, and you'll feel confident the next time you play the sport.

But what does this say to be assertive? If your subconscious mind continues to find that others are violating your rights and you never stand up for them, your self-confidence can diminish. On the other side, when you hold your subconscious mind behaving assertively, you will feel that you are capable, and you will become more relaxed.

How to become assertive and confident To become assertive, you need to:

Stand up for your rights whenever they are abused.

Using positive body language (straight back, relaxed hands and no arms crossed)

It would help if you used "I" expression to be sure, for instance, "I can't see why you'd like to take it off".

ACCEPTANCE AND FORGIVENESS OF YOUR MISTAKES

Making mistakes doesn't feel good in any context. Whether you say the wrong thing during an argument or don't meet a deadline at work, it is easy to label or see yourself as a bad person or say you are not good enough. However, regardless of how hard people try in their lives, there is not one single perfect person. Human beings have complex minds and emotions. Even once you learn to control your emotions, there will be times when you mess up. It is not the mistake that matters, however. It is what you do after the mistake. This will guide you in what to do following a mistake, so you can react in a way that reflects your self-love and benefits your future.

Realizing That Mistakes Are Normal

Think back to a time when a role model made a mistake. It may have been a parent or a relative, or a celebrity that was involved in some scandal. When these people that we idolize make mistakes, it is often blown out of proportion. It can be disappointing, shocking, and even discouraging to realize someone that you admire so much makes a mistake. However, what these shocking situations represent is the reality that even the people we look up to make mistakes.

Accepting that mistakes are normal is critical to growing confidence and self-esteem. Someone who cannot accept their mistakes will feel bad about themselves every time they mess up. While there is nothing wrong with experiencing a negative emotion, especially if it is a severe mistake, dwelling on it does more harm than good. Think about what you have learned about positive thinking so far. By thinking negatively about yourself, you are not harming anyone but yourself.

Gaining Perspective on Mistakes

When people make mistakes, one of the biggest questions they have is, "Why?" They may want to know why they can't be normal or why they can't stop messing things up. Mistakes happen for any number of reasons—here's a look at a few of them.

- You are on auto-pilot. Humans are habitual creatures. The brain is constantly busy, trying to keep everything running smoothly in your body. To reduce stress and the number of tasks that the brain needs to focus on, it goes into auto-pilot mode. This is where conscious thought switches off, and you begin doing what you would normally do, but with minimal effort. This is the reason that your drive to work in the morning seems natural and effortless—and the reason you turn onto the wrong exit on the freeway is taking your child to soccer practice when your brain is taking you to work. Even though these habitual practices are helpful, they can cause you to make mistakes. When you are constantly making mistakes on autopilot, you can try mindfulness exercises to help keep you at the moment.

- You are experiencing strong emotions. People are most likely to act irrationally when they are upset. When you are sad and hungry, you are more likely to lip up on your diet. When you are angry with someone, you are more likely to argue with them or say mean things. This is natural when you are experiencing a particularly strong surge of emotions. You can learn to manage your emotions better with some of the strategies we'll discuss later. Nevertheless, take note that there may be some highly emotional situations where you might struggle to put your skills to use.

- You lack experience. People are especially prone to mistakes when they are trying something new. This is not something that you should ever see as discouragement. After all, no one on this planet is skilled at everything. When you do fail, remember that you have learned what not to do. This brings you closer to having the experience you need to carry out the task flawlessly. Research shows that it takes ten years for someone to become an expert in some areas. If you are worried you are behind on the curve, do some research and use that to set goals for yourself.

- You are not taking care of yourself. People are more likely to create mistakes or act irrationally when they are tired, hungry, or stressed. You must get the proper amount of sleep each night and make an effort to eat well and find time to relax. When you do not care and are not taking care of yourself, you are more prone to making mistakes. This means more time spent fixing the problem and even less time taking care of yourself.

The Difference between Mistakes and Bad Decisions

You cannot excuse every undesirable outcome that you make in life as the result of a mistake. It is not a mistake to stay up late watching our favorite television show instead of resting because you have a test tomorrow—it is a bad decision. Taking the scenic route to a meeting when you are already late is a bad decision, not an honest mistake.

Another critical difference between mistakes and bad decisions is how you should handle them. Both must be dealt with if you are to continue working toward your goals and becoming the best person you can be. However, when you make bad decisions, pay closer attention to what you are doing. Bad decisions are a form of self-sabotage, where you consciously decide to make things harder in your life. You may find the allure of self-sabotage declines as you increase your self-esteem and begin living your best life.

The Positive Side of Mistakes

Every mistake is an opportunity to learn. Someone cooking bacon for the first time might turn the pan up on high heat because they want the bacon crispy. However, by setting a higher heat, the bacon sticks to the pan, and the grease starts flying everywhere. The bacon does not get crispy—it burns. Yes, it is a fact that this is a little mistake, but it is one that teaches that bacon should be cooked on medium heat rather than turning it to a high temperature. The next time that person goes to cook bacon, they will adjust the heat accordingly. They know to do this because they made a mistake in the first place.

Every mistake is a critical learning lesson. It should not be categorized as a problem—but as a time to re-evaluate. If someone says something hurtful when they are angry in an argument, they might regret it later. This regret is better spent evaluating where they went wrong. They may want to consider the strong emotions tied to their anger and the triggers that caused them to become that upset. If they had an outburst because they had been bottling something up for a while, they might need to re-evaluate the way they address problems or the way they express their emotions.

A major benefit of learning to accept and learn from mistakes is that you gain the confidence to try new things. People who are perfectionists do not try something unless they are absolutely positive they will succeed at it. However, this holds them back from attempting things they are unsure of. They may not try new things or complete projects because they do not have the confidence to follow through.

Why Forgiving Your Own Mistakes is Important?

Imagine for a moment that you are walking up a staircase. This staircase represents the path to a goal. While you are walking up the staircase, somewhere around the middle, you have a misstep. Now, what do you do? Would you get back up and keep moving forward? Or would you throw yourself down the stairs and sabotage all the progress you have made in meeting your goal?

When you do not forgive yourself for your mistakes, you are self-sabotaging. Mistakes can bring about feelings of sadness, disappointment, anger, and guilt. These feelings are all negative and unpleasant. While experiencing them after a mistake is natural, continuing to dwell on them only punishes you. When you make a mistake and refuse to let go of it, you are causing yourself pain and other negative emotions for no reason other than to sabotage yourself.

Remember that you are only human. Expect yourself to make mistakes. No breathing person has never made a mistake in their lives. People make mistakes from the time they are young, and all they do is continue to learn from them. Think about the number of cups that a toddler might spill before they finally manage to drink out of a cup. These cups are all mistakes—but without making those mistakes, that toddler never would have been successful in drinking out of a cup.

Strategies for Forgiving Yourself

- Forgiveness is something easier said than done. While it gets easier to forgive yourself (and others), the more you practice, it is challenging at first. These strategies might make letting go of your mistakes easier:

- Separate yourself from your past. Every person's past is a unique story, some of them darker than others. When mistakes are lingering around from your past, the best way to forgive yourself is to focus on change. If you are so upset with your behavior that it is plaguing you now, try separating yourself from your past. Take not at any moment in time, and you have the choice and power to change the way you do things and become a better person. You cannot achieve this if you are constantly looking back, obsessed with the person you once were. Instead, become a better version of yourself.

- Credit your strengths. Giving yourself a confidence boost after you have made a mistake helps you celebrate your strengths and balance your weaknesses. This works best at times when you have excelled at something but made a mistake in a similar area. For example, while a person might fail at cooking bacon the first time, they might have a really good palate and be good at combining spices. They are not horrible at cooking altogether—they just need a little more practice in some areas.

- Mistakes are always present and part of any learning process. Forgiveness is important because it can be detrimental to trust your judgment too much. Research shows that people who are experts in their fields (like doctors) are less likely to catch and correct mistakes because they believe their judgment is solid. When you are open to mistakes, it gives you a better chance of identifying and remedying them before they become a major problem. Additionally, by being open to mistakes, you are giving yourself a chance to explore your self-confidence without stressing over setbacks.

- Approach with an experimental attitude. When you are trying something new, it can be high-pressure, or it can be fun. Instead of stressing over if you will do something right, make it an experiment. Take a yoga class or work with a high-profile client, just to see what happens. Even though failure may be an option, it is much more likely that it will result in a learning experience.

- Shut out the critics. Sometimes, the mistakes we make leave us being held accountable by other people. When you cannot convince someone to forgive for your mistakes, it is still important to forgive yourself. Holding onto grudges does little to invite positivity into your life. Instead of worrying about how society is reacting, remember that you are a work-in-progress. Making mistakes is natural, and those people who expect you to be perfect are the type of people that only add stress to your life.

WHEN THINGS GO WRONG, SHIFT TO LOVE

Love is the antidote to everything.

Love means something different to everyone. So you understand how we're using love in this context, we're looking at Love vs. Fear.

Biologically, our brains are wired for fear. It's the way we used to survive, literally, by looking for the next shoe—or next spear—to drop. The reptilian brain includes the brainstem and the cerebellum, which are reliable but tend to be somewhat rigid and compulsive, hence the name 'reptilian.' Now, in modern times, without the daily fear of death, our brains transfer that 'fear scanning' to less deadly things, like money woes, or if that next latte will be hot enough, or how bad the traffic will be.

Fear is only useful when making life or death decisions in the moment.

In short order, fear is not serving you at all. It's hurting you. That's the time to shift to love.

When real tragedy strikes, that's another issue altogether. A death. An accident. A large loss of some kind. I'm not saying ignore the feelings that come up, and I'm saying think of something that represents love— a person, a thing, or a memory—and hold that image in your head to help replace the fear and awful feelings. It's good to feel your feelings (good or not so good). It is through our feelings that we know what direction to head. When you are at an uncomfortable fork in the road, the best course is choosing love; especially when things don't feel good. Slowly, and over time, you will learn how to use those good thoughts more effectively.

It takes an intentional human to shift to love.

You can do it! When the trigger appears, that is opportunity knocking on your spiritual door. Are you going to answer it with LOVE? Or

Fear? Ask yourself, what would LOVE do at this moment? And if I represent love, what would love to do?

Emotionally, love is the antidote and cancels out fear, so it takes the electric charge out of that 'fight or flight' knee-jerk reaction our reptilian brains have and therefore facilitates inner-peace. And the outcome will probably be better. Whatever decision-making processes you need to go through will be more measured, calm, and logical if you can get away from the bad emotional reaction.

Without fear, or ego involved, things become more manageable; more approachable.

Ask yourself, what am I gaining by emotional hand-wringing, holding onto fear, anguish, or anxiety? Why am I letting THAT take up valuable real estate in my head? Allow love to take its place. Let go of the inner censor. Stick a toe into the world of love and see how it feels.

Think of love as that eternal and infinite compass that resides in you. It's that place within that tells you who you are, what is best for you, and shows you the way to healthier and better choices. When you tap into it, you tap into the universal flow.

We are all creators. It's time to design and construct a new choice.

Every journey starts with awareness. Awareness transforms into Becoming. From Point A to Point B is an imaginary line that only you can draw. How will you travel? I hope with a new awareness of love and its powerful transformative properties.

"True life is lived when tiny changes occur."

Practice. Practice. Practice. Create space for yourself to do just that. Silence the Critic and just feel. Emotions are the key to your destiny. They fuel your life and drive your choices. So, practice shifting to the universal and healing emotion of love. Fear will pass more quickly, like a cold breeze. Then, the sun will find you, and you can embrace the rays. Like the sun, love will warm you and radiate out to others. Once you shift to love, you will feel like you've captured lightning in a bottle…and you have!

PLANNING YOUR FUTURE

Before you start working on creating the future, you need to determine what you want in life. Think about the three key aspects of your life-your physical and mental well-being, job or career, and relationships. Have a rest and take time and think about the different things you wish to attain in each of these aspects. You probably want to improve your overall health or lose weight. Maybe you want to change your job or get a promotion at work. Perhaps you are interested in letting go of certain toxic relationships and working on nurturing and developing healthy relationships.

Whatever it is, spend the necessary time, and start visualizing the kind of future you want. Sit down and think, and don't worry about anything else. Try to make your visualization as detailed as you possibly can, and it will add more meaning to it. Once you complete this exercise, start to note down all the points included in your visualization. When you set up a certain goal, it becomes easier to take the required action to achieve that goal. Make a shortlist of all your goals, long-term and short-term goals. These goals will act as homing beacons to ensure you are on the right path. Also, when you start working with a goal in mind, you can be more effective and efficient.

While setting goals for your future, ensure that the goals are small, measurable, attainable, realistic, and time-bound. Don't make your goals vague and make them specific. For example, "I want to earn a lot of money without doing anything," is a vague goal. Instead, "I want to increase my earnings by 24% within the next eight months," is an example of a specific goal.

Keep in mind that all the tips given need to be followed with some consistency. As mentioned, self-discovery is an ongoing process, and it isn't a destination. You need to keep following the simple practices you have developed if you want to make the most of your life. Keep working on improving and understanding yourself, and you will become a force to be reckoned with.

Always keep your self-discovery journal with you. Whenever you are running low on motivation, go through the different things you have discovered about yourself to feel better. Life has plenty to offer, provided you are willing to look at it objectively! Once you understand yourself, you will know what you want and don't want to. This kind of knowledge certainly helps put things in perspective and bring about a sense of clarity. When all these factors are integrated together, you can lead a happy life without any regrets.

Self-Acceptance

Do you accept yourself despite your flaws?

Self-discovery will teach you to love and accept yourself unconditionally. It's easy to love something flawless, but to love even when flawed is unconditional and true love.

The simplest way in which you can practice self-acceptance is to be kind and compassionate toward yourself. You are your worst critic and always keep that in mind, and no one can judge you any harsher or than you already do. Be patient and kind, not just with others, but yourself too. Always face your fears head-on, and don't try to hide them in the deep recess of your mind. Once you confront your fears, they don't have any power over you. Let go of any preconceived notions of perfection you have in mind. Chasing perfection is a fool's errand. Instead, work on attaining your goals and embrace your imperfections.

Regardless of what happens, the one thing you can always manage is your attitude. Your attitude is based on your thoughts. It's quite easy to feel pessimistic but try to be more optimistic. When you keep a positive attitude towards life, even when stuck in trouble, it becomes easier to think clearly. The ability to forgive oneself and others will work in your favor in all aspects of your life. If you make a mistake, learn your lessons from it, and move on. Don't beat yourself up for things you cannot change. Forgive others for what they did, and your heart will feel lighter. Never stop believing in yourself and don't give up. Self-acceptance takes time and effort, but the results will be worth your while.

Manage your Time and Finances

Do you think you manage your time and finances properly?

Self-discovery brings with it an awareness of how you manage your limited resources, especially time and your finances. The time that goes by doesn't come back. Likewise, if you are careless, you will soon be neck-deep in debt that is difficult to get out of. To avoid this, it is important to learn to manage these resources. In addition to what we've covered earlier in this workbook, here are some more effective ways to manage your time and money.

Start by eliminating all the unnecessary routines from your life. You don't have to waste 45 minutes on social media daily, and you certainly don't have to stick to unnecessary calls on the phone for two hours. Prioritize all the tasks in order of their importance and get rid of anything that doesn't seem necessary. When you eliminate the unnecessary, you finally have sufficient time to concentrate on things that matter. Like we've mentioned, avoid multitasking whenever possible. It's a myth to think we can focus on more than one thing at a time. When you multitask, your overall productivity doesn't increase, but it decreases. Even if it feels like you're getting more things done, you aren't. Always plan the work you wish to accomplish within a given timeframe. Avoid distractions and interruptions while at work. Not just work, but with any task you wish to perform too.

There are few reminders on how you can manage your finances. Always create a budget. When you have a budget, you know when to stop spending. Plan your expenses based on your income. Don't overestimate your earning capacity and never underestimate your expenses. Take stock of your overall debt level and try to clear it as soon as possible. Start planning for your retirement and always create an emergency fund. The emergency fund should be able to sustain you for at least 5 to 6 months.

General Perspective

What do you feel about your general outlook in life?

It's been mentioned repeatedly in this book that your perspective towards life matters a lot. Yes, it does matter because everything you do is based on your perception of reality. If your perspective is tinted with unnecessary negativity, you cannot see an opportunity, even when it is staring you right in the face. Therefore, put in some effort and change your overall outlook toward life.

To quickly summarize and review, ensure that you get sufficient sleep at night. When your body and mind are well-rested, your overall mood improves. When your spirits are high, it becomes easier to maintain a positive outlook. Spend at least 30 minutes, indulging in a simple self-care routine. Learn to practice forgiveness. Forgive not just yourself, but others too. Make sure your body gets sufficient exercise; it needs to stay healthy and fit. Don't ignore your loved ones, and try to make more time for them. Avoid toxic relationships and concentrate on surrounding yourself with people who bring happiness and positivity into your life. Learn to seek happiness within yourself and don't associate it with worldly possessions.

Health Matters

Are there any aspects of your overall well-being you would want to work on? Do you think you are in perfect health? If not, then what aspects of your health would you want to improve?

Remember, take some time and carefully think about all these three questions. Take care of your physical, mental, and emotional health. You cannot function effectively and efficiently if there is an imbalance in any of these three aspects of your life. To do this, you need to concentrate on consuming a healthy diet, getting sufficient sleep, and exercise. By following these three simple exercises, you can significantly improve your physical health. When in good physical health, it improves your mood. When your mood is better, your mental health improves. In order to enhance your mental health, take time for self-reflection, learn to manage your stress, and understand and accept your thoughts. To increase and improve your emotional health, start by accepting your emotions, analyze the reason for these emotions, and work to express them positively.

Nourish Your Relationships

What do you feel about all the different relationships in your life?

Do you want to develop and nourish healthy relationships?

Relationships matter a lot in your life. Yes, you can work hard to achieve success, but usually, there are plenty of others who help you along the way. This help can be direct or indirect. Keep in mind that human beings are social animals. You cannot cut yourself off from your social circle entirely. Maintaining healthy and positive relationships are essential for your mental and emotional well-being. For instance, how do you feel when you are around people who support and love you unconditionally? You will feel better about yourself.

Likewise, you might notice, certain people drain you of your energy and make you feel low. Start analyzing the different relationships in your life and prioritize the healthy ones. If you notice any toxic relationships, it is time to break free of the toxicity and move away. The best method to perform this is to set boundaries for yourself. Your personal boundaries are not just a sign of your self-respect and self-love, but it helps you understand what is and isn't desirable in your life.

Your Professional Life

What do you desire from your professional life? Do you like your job? What are your ambitions? Do you want to change anything about your professional life?

Spend some time for self-reflection and carefully answer these questions. On average, you might work for about 7 to 9 hours on any given day. That's more than one-third of your life dedicated to work. Therefore, it is important to ensure that your work is something you are passionate about. If you don't like your work or aren't interested in it, then it is difficult to set any goals, as the chances of you giving up on your career increases. To avoid this, it is quintessential that your work and passions are in sync. When you truly enjoy your work, you can excel in it.

Set Some Goals

Have you set any goals for yourself?

When you set certain goals for yourself, it lends a sense of purpose and direction. When you know all the effort you make pushes you towards a result you desire, your motivation to keep working increases. Goals can be set in any aspect of your life and don't have to be restricted to your professional life. There are a variety of goals you can set depending on what you wish to attain. From personal, health, relationships, and career, there are plenty of goals you can set.

POSITIVE SELF-TALK FOR PRODUCTIVITY HACK

Self-talk is the process of either speaking verbally or mentally about oneself. No matter how positive or negative, these are the things you're sending yourself about yourself all day long. You will be empowered by the things that you send yourself, or they will hinder you if they're pessimistic.

For example, if you attend a work party and crack a joke in front of ten peers and no one really laughs, only a few chuckles from some that are good, what should you do after the party about yourself? Do you drive home saying, "I should have just held my mouth shut, maybe they think I'm a fool," or should you say to yourself, "No big deal, at least I've put myself out there and done it." You may also hesitate from revealing too much out of fear of humiliation or leaving you feeling terrible. Worse still, if you feel insecure about your relationships with others, you can grow an aversion to social circumstances.

Self-talk version two helps you to grant yourself a pass to start again, to just be alive, and to communicate with others. We can't always be 100 percent all the time on the mark for laughter and social experiences, but at least striving is worth the effort.

Self-talking is so crucial that these are the signals which decide whether or not you should keep attempting. Whether the messages you deliver will help you excel, or they will pull you down and leave you crippled in terror.

8 possible ways to achieve positive self-talk for success and productivity

1. Have a Purpose Higher Than Self

Having deep confidence in a higher power makes positive self-talk helpful. Data shows that teenagers who have "daily religious service participation, strong contextual religion value, and years spent in

Christian youth activities are correlated with better self-esteem and more optimistic self-attitudes." Maintaining confidence in a greater entity, along with engagement in a religious society, allows people to have higher self-esteem. Self-esteem and speak about oneself go hand in hand. For example, if you assume that God (or some higher power) is good and loves you, then your emotions against yourself are going to be childlike. You were formed to a reason by a higher being who produced you. You are more likely to trust in yourself when you trust this in your bones and seek the good stuff you are made for in life.

When you believe you have meaning, you're focused on the good things you've been made to follow and accomplish.

2. Cut Overly Negative People out of Your Life

Anyone may be moody or pessimistic and have a poor day. Many other people tend to get poor days every day of their lives. When you have some of those individuals in your life, perhaps it might be wise to separate yourself from them.

People's behavior about you can influence your behaviors. If anyone has a depressive outlook, it is possible that those around them may be brought down, particularly if their sadness is chronic over time and in a variety of circumstances.

It isn't easy to take relatives or friends out of your life. You'll also be limiting your time and exposure to these men. Don't spend energy interacting with derogative collaborators. Do not stay in for hostile co-workers in the breakroom. Keep the tension to a minimum in your life by reducing your contact with the negative people.

3. Be Grateful

Considering the things, you would be thankful for in your life is a great way to find the positivity in your life, and build positive self-talk. Finding things in your daily life that you are thankful for helps improve your attitude and will encourage you to have a healthier, more positive self-talk.

One way to show gratitude is by generating a gratitude survey. Using it to write things you're happy for every day.

Some of the things will be growing, and some will be small. This will help you reflect on the good things that are occurring in your life, particularly when it was as simple as seeing a sunset or spending time walking and talking with a friend.

In a document, the representation of your thanks makes certain feelings and memories more real. You make yourself rely on the happiness of your world.

It doesn't even need to be a long-winded post. You may only start by taking a journal and enumerating 3 to 5 things at the end of each day for which you are grateful for that specific day.

4. Don't Compare Yourself to Others

You easily down yourself when you are continually comparing what you want to what others have.

When you're playing the game of comparison, it's easy to feel negative about your life. Just have gratitude in what you have, instead of dwelling on what you do not have.

You might have a casual mate, for example, who also gets a new car every two years. They are usually top of the line, beautiful vehicles. On the other side, you are driving a minivan, which is ten years old. You have children of the same generation, the same history in schooling, and you are both married to successful spouses. You equate yourself to what she has and ask if every year you can not get a new car, too.

What you don't realize is that she and her husband are in major debt. We don't work beyond their means, so expected too least to retire. You and your partner were very responsible for managing the expenses and retirements.

Comparing yourself to someone else isn't smart since you don't know the whole story.

You will still consider someone better off than you, or worse off. Concentrating on oneself and being thankful for one's life is more significant. Live your existence, and make no distinctions.

5. Use Positive Words with Others

If we are pessimistic about other people's words, then we are likely to be pessimistic towards ourselves too. Poor emotions lead to negative self-talk. When you realize you're in a rut of misery, then quit immediately. Start communicating with the people in your life about life and affirming something you care about, even yourself. Doing that will make the core change its disposition.

For example, will you start your first discussion when you get to work in the morning by moaning about all the stuff that went wrong in your morning? Or are you happy that the sun is rising and you have a work of covering the bills and voicing such feelings to your colleagues?

What's coming out of the mouth may be optimistic or bad. You have the option. When you've picked the bad, that won't add something good to your day or life. Another consideration is how we treat others we care about. Should you continuously nag your spouse or friend or find fault? But are you concentrating on the optimistic and saying inspiring words to them?

When you catch yourself concentrating on the dishes left in the tub, putting them on the floor with wet towels, and refusing to walk the dog again, you'll say these terms to your loved one.

If you speak to your loved ones about discontent, nagging, and guilt, they start feeling pessimistic about you. Their response to you will definitely not be good. They would undoubtedly react with a sarcastic comment such as "you'll still nag me" or "you'll never help with the laundry."

When you will let go of the negative stuff and then concentrate on the good and use uplifting terms, that can make your home life much better. Tell "thank you for putting out the garbage," for starters, and "thank you for helping to put the children to bed." Also, if you intend them to do certain stuff, receiving a compliment and words of affirmation always feels amazing. In addition, such optimistic phrases would carry good thoughts and potentially more positive behavior from them.

Due to your insistence on their constructive acts, the interactions can become more optimistic. Your ability to take the time to consider these issues and give support and gratitude orally would reinforce the relationships.

Positivity produces positively, and negative creates negatively. Take the one that is better for you and others.

6. Believe in Your Success

Believe in how good you are. Believe in the abilities you have so that you can propel yourself into success. Doubting yourself prevents you from attempting, and so stops you from achieving. Believe you will be effective, even if several attempts are necessary.

For example, if you go to a fitness class and you've already convinced yourself that you will definitely not be able to finish it, then you're going to struggle. When you head through a scenario emotionally convincing yourself that you cannot or may not be able to carry out the mission at hand successfully, you set yourself up for failure.

Stick to convincing yourself you should. And if you decide to change your steps to get moving, remind yourself you're not going to stop. Tell yourself you'll get the work done one way or another. You have to remind yourself that you will achieve what you intend to do and that you can excel at anything you bring your attention to. If you don't trust in yourself, who will then?

7. Don't Fear Failure

Never be scared of defeat, as that is always the path to success. Many of life's best success stories are about individuals who struggled several times before they were successful. If they had given up after losing for the first time, then they would never have been hugely successful. Fear of disappointment is holding many people off from really attempting to achieve. They remain in their lifetime status quo, so they exist in fear of defeat.

Don't let anxiety prevent you from attempting. Tell yourself if you fall, you should keep trying! If you blast a job project, for example, don't convince yourself you're a loser. Look at it more as a chance to discover a different way to move on with the project and develop in your ability set.

Don't carry in and acknowledge the loss. Instead, reframe the encounter as an incentive to learn and improve further of whatever work you do. Do not toss your old work out if someone refused it. Perhaps you need it later. Place it sideways and save for future use. You never knew whether a project that wasn't successful for that instance would succeed for another. When you look at a loss as an incentive to start harder and pursue a new path, your attempts aren't futile.

8. Replace Negative Thoughts with Positive Ones

Negative thoughts do exist. It's hard to hold optimistic thoughts about yourself all the time. But you will start replacing the good thinking with the bad ones. There is also the other side of each case, even upside down. It is up to you to keep seeing the good and continue transforming the positives into constructive ones. For example, whether you're prone to convince yourself you're overweight, you're going to feel overweight and bad about the way you look. If you aren't obese, so quit sending this word to yourself!

If you are overweight but strive to enhance your overall fitness, then concentrate your mind on those feelings. When it comes to your mind that you appear obese when washing your hands at the mirror in the shower, instantly erase those feelings. Rather, reassure yourself that you are trying to bring in meaningful improvements in your body and are taking every day moves towards becoming healthy.

Tell yourself that you are pleased with yourself, as you are taking daily attempts to change what you think needs to be changed. When you have your exercises done, tell "job well completed."

CONCLUSION: I LOVE ME

Creating lasting and impactful changes in how we feel and the lives we lead is about the things we do consistently. Commitment is key here. You can't expect to go to the gym once and get the body of Victoria's Secret's model. In the same sense, you cannot expect to meditate once and for your life to transform overnight. Transforming your inner world so that you shape your outer world can be easy, and it can be quick, but first, you've got to create a little bit of forwarding momentum. Think of it as a snowball effect. You start with baby steps towards a small, easy to reach the goal.

Choose a goal right now, in which you have a relatively strong belief that it is possible for you. Once you start to witness these mini manifestations appear, you strengthen your belief that you are being supported. You begin to feel more confident in who you are and your abilities to create the life you want, and from this place, things get better and better.

Starting with small goals and desires doesn't mean you are limiting yourself or settling, but you are using your smaller goals as a test to prove to yourself that this process works. So let's say you're looking to manifest a lump sum of money. To begin with, this could be a relatively low amount. When you are working with a smaller manifestation, it's far easier to create the belief that it is possible for you. You are much more likely to expect it to appear. Then, once you receive that money and thank The Universe for providing you with your desires, the next time around, you can set your sights higher.

Sometimes, it's so easy to become focused on the huge lofty goals we forget about the smaller stuff that could equally bring us a lot of joy. While we may want to manifest millions in the bank, the dream home, the successful business, or a soulmate, think of something you'd like more of right now that feels within reach. I've manifested lots of little things along the way, things which may have not totally overhauled my life in one go, but have edged me closer and closer to the life I want.

I will often see the whole manifesting process as a fun game I'm playing with The Universe. Sometimes I'll ask myself, "what can I co-create today with The Universe?" before deciding on what I'd like more of and seeing what shows up. The quickest way to get to the bigger manifestation is to use these smaller desires as your stepping stones. Use these smaller desires as your fuel to raise your frequency and strengthen your faith in The Universe and, before you know it, things will have escalated into bigger and better things. In time, things will happen quicker, perhaps even instantaneously.

Exercise - Manifest a small gift from The Universe.

Set an intention to receive a small gift from The Universe over the next week. For example, let's say you decide to manifest a free cup of coffee. Use the Self Love & Spiritual Alchemy Process to manifest this desire.

Write down your desire in your daily journal. Pin a picture of this desire to your vision board.

Understand what is holding you back from having this in your possession right now? What beliefs are you holding onto that make you think you don't deserve to get something for anything? Where are you perhaps still doubting that The Universe will support you in this desire?

Transform your beliefs to help you believe that what you want is already yours.

Create an affirmation expressing your thanks for its arrival as if it is already in your possession. For example, "I'm so happy and grateful I have received this free cup of coffee." Create an affirmation around how you deserve to receive things for free. For example, "I deserve to receive things for free." Create an affirmation to help you strengthen your belief in The Universe. For example, "When I ask for something, The Universe always delivers."

Transform your energy so that you become a vibrational match to your desires. How would it feel if anything you wanted could show up into your life for free? Sit for a while in silence and imagine a whole21 week where people just gave you whatever you asked for without needing to pay for it. How does that make you feel? Enhance your vibration by performing the things that lift you higher. Spend time with those who bring you joy. Make space for self-care.

Take inspired action towards your desire. What can you do that maximizes your chances of your desire coming into existence? Visit your local coffee, for example.

Surrender and let go. Trust that The Universe is going to give you   this gift at exactly the moment you are meant to receive it, and it will be what you've asked for OR something better. Know that whatever you receive this week will be in your highest interests.

Rather than wondering, "when is my free coffee going to appear?!", expect it to show up at any time and, in the meantime, enjoy your life as much as possible without stressing too much about whether it will or won't show up.

Activate your Feminine Energy. Get yourself into alignment by tapping into your feminine power. To receive something for free, you have to be in the receptive mode. Ask yourself where else in your life could you allow yourself to receive a little more?

Maybe it's someone helping you in the house or with your children. Maybe it's asking for more support at work.

At the end of the week, journal what amazing things you have witnessed. Perhaps you will receive a cup of coffee. Or maybe not.

Maybe, The Universe has decided to send something even better your way. Make a note of how you feel at the end of this exercise, too, because ultimately, the reason why we want to have anything is that we want to feel better.

Have you noticed a difference in how you feel through doing this exercise? What is important with this is that you have fun with this process. It's supposed to feel light and easy and enjoyable. It's just a free cup of coffee, after all.

This is the beauty of starting this process with something small. There isn't too much fear around this type of desire. It doesn't feel as daunting as manifesting some of the bigger stuff. It's easy to think of the manifesting process as a fun game. It's the bigger goals that normally come with more resistance and require deeper transformations.

When it comes to displaying some of your loftier desires, the shifts you must go through can feel uncomfortable, to begin with. When there is real healing to be done, a lot of fears to work through, a lot of limiting beliefs to change, and a lot of negative energy you are holding onto, the beginning of the process can feel a little bit challenging. Stick with it. On the other side of this work, you will realize that things just flow. Things are and always will be working out for you, but to begin with, you may need to clear the path of a lot of junk so that you can allow things in.

Close your eyes and imagine you are standing on the edge of a forest. On the other side of the forest is everything you've ever wanted; The life you want to live, the career you are passionate about, the money in the bank, the dream house, the dreamboat of a soul mate, the healthy, vibrant body. Anything you've ever wished for is there, waiting for you. From where you are right now, you can't see these things physically. You just have to trust that they are there. The only thing that is preventing you from your path is those trees. It's up to you to navigate your way through them.

To begin with, the trees are close together. It's dark. Sometimes you stumble. Sometimes you doubt whether you are moving in the right direction. You know however, that once you get to the other side, it will all be worth it. As you continue to explore the forest, you begin to notice the trees becoming sparser and the light beginning to creep in. Your path becomes easier to navigate, and the further you go, the lighter things become. Things begin to feel easier, and you are able to move quickly, and then, seemingly out of nowhere, the forest just opens up. You have arrived.

Starting out on this path, it is sometimes difficult to see the light through the trees, but you have to have faith that what you want is waiting for you. The trees are your mindset, and once you learn how to navigate your inner world, things become easier. Then, eventually, you will realize that there is absolutely nothing standing in your way. You are more powerful than what you give yourself credit for. You do not need someone to clear down the trees for you.

You've got everything you need within you right now. This process is not about becoming someone you are not, but tapping into the unique treasures within you that you didn't even realize you possess, treasures you've buried away that are just waiting to be discovered.

Confidence, self-belief, resilience, worthiness, deservedness, tenacity, faith, optimism - You have all of the things within you at your disposal and, when you figure out how to unleash them, you will realize that the life you are meant for has been yours for the taking all along.

I'd like to finish with a reminder that life doesn't happen to you. It happens because of you. You have the power over what you experience. How you feel, who you allow yourself to be, what you create, the people you attract, and the life that you design are up to you.

Life also is happening for you, even in the moments when you feel that it isn't the case. There is always a reason why The Universe allows things to unfold the way that they do, and it will always serve your best interests in the long run. It may not make sense, to begin with, but soon you will realize that every road bumps you go through, you grow through, and within every wrong turn, there are lessons we need to help us blossom into the women we are meant to be.

When you fully commit to this work and begin to witness all of life's little miracles along the way, miracles that you have co-created, you will realize that there are no limits in life apart from the limits we place on ourselves.

The biggest act of Self Love happens when you choose to break free of those limits.

So, my darling, I invite you now to do just that. Break free of those limits and run like wildfire towards the life you are meant for.

You are worth it.

www.ingramcontent.com/pod-product-compliance
Lightning Source LLC
Chambersburg PA
CBHW070808240726
48654CB00007B/261